Number Fourteen
Carolyn and Ernest Fay Series in Analytical Psychology

David H. Rosen, General Editor

The Carolyn and Ernest Fay edited book series, based initially on the annual Fay Lecture Series in Analytical Psychology, was established to further the ideas of C. G. Jung among students, faculty, therapists, and other citizens and to enhance scholarly activities related to analytical psychology. The Book Series and Lecture Series address topics of importance to the individual and to society. Both series were generously endowed by Carolyn Grant Fay, the founding president of the C. G. Jung Educational Center in Houston, Texas. The series are in part a memorial to her late husband, Ernest Bel Fay. Carolyn Fay has planted a Jungian tree carrying both her name and that of her late husband, which will bear fruitful ideas and stimulate creative works from this time forward. Texas A&M University and all those who come in contact with the growing Fay Jungian tree are extremely grateful to Carolyn Grant Fay for what she has done. The holder of the McMillan Professorship in Analytical Psychology at Texas A&M functions as the general editor of the Fay Book Series.

The Therapeutic Relationship

The Therapeutic Relationship

Transference, Countertransference, and the Making of Meaning

JAN WIENER

Foreword by David H. Rosen

Texas A&M University Press • College Station

This paper meets the requirements of ANSI/NISO Z39.48-1992
(Permanence of Paper).
Binding materials have been chosen for durability.

LIBRARY OF CONGRESS CATALOGING-IN-PUBLICATION DATA

Wiener, Jan.
The therapeutic relationship : transference, countertransference, and the
making of meaning / Jan Wiener ; foreword by David H. Rosen. — 1st ed.
p. cm. — (Carolyn and Ernest Fay series in analytical psychology ; no. 14)
Includes bibliographical references and index.
ISBN-13: 978-1-60344-147-6 (cloth : alk. paper)
ISBN-10: 1-60344-147-6 (cloth : alk. paper)
1. Transference (Psychology). 2. Countertransference (Psychology).
3. Psychotherapist and patient. 4. Jungian psychology. I. Title. II. Series:
Carolyn and Ernest Fay series in analytical psychology ; no. 14.
RC489.T73.W45 2009
616.89'17—dc22
2009010424

Contents

Series Editor's Foreword

Between doctor and patient, there are imponderable
factors which bring about a mutual transformation.

—C. G. Jung

Jan Wiener has written a scholarly, creative, and integrative volume that acknowledges the imponderable but focuses on the perceptible factors in the therapeutic relationship. She explores the significance of the processes of transference and countertransference for the therapeutic relationship. She also gives careful consideration to multiple aspects involved in transference and countertransference, as well as the way in which they contribute to the making of meaning in the healing relationship of therapy and analysis. Her book involves unusual depth (symbols from archetypal dreams and myths) and breadth (relational moments of purpose and significance) in examining transference and countertransference. A member of the Society of Analytical Psychology (SAP) in London, Jan Wiener sheds light on transference and countertransference in historical and developmental ways. In addition, she investigates areas in which what we know about transference and countertransference in the field of analytical psychology dovetails well with psychoanalysis and other areas in which it does not. Fortunately, her muse also takes her to both old and new frontiers from Jung's alchemical approach to neurobiology and therefore makes this text beneficial to a wide range of analytic and therapeutic perspectives. In other words, a member of the SAP, other Jungian analytic associations, a Freudian psychoanalytic society, or any psychotherapy group could learn much and find meaning in this volume.

Jan Wiener is a singer, as well as an analyst, and it is clear from her clinical examples that she achieves attunement with her patients.[1] She deals with tangibles head on: learning notes and techniques before improvising, which she does at times with boldness. For example, she proposes a "transference matrix" as the fertile ground for meaning to creatively emerge in the therapeutic relationship. The writing reveals an admirable honesty and integrity, along with a deep respect for the poetic and imaginal. Jan Wiener also displays an equanimity that involves a balance of transference and countertransference in her relationships with patients; this dance of subjective and objective realms allows for healing at both the unconscious and the conscious levels of the psyche. Moreover, meaning evolves from the imponderable factors, which are—in the end—mysterious and lead to mutual transformation. She even considers countertransference, particularly its intersubjectivity on a collective unconscious level, a form of creative active imagination. Hers is a contemporary work that brings in research evidence from other fields (science, philosophy, and the arts) to the therapeutic relationship and the making of meaning.

Jan Wiener reflects on transference and reveals how she both "works in" and "works with" it. Her last chapter, "Transference for Life: Keeping the Patient in Mind," mirrors a valuable maxim for all who participate in therapy. I would like to add the perspective of soul and suggest that our woundedness is a critical part of our becoming analysts and wounded healers. An ethics of awareness regarding one's own wounds and the implications for countertransference are paramount. By being wounded analytic researchers, which is what analysis and therapy is all about, we help our patients heal their own pain through analytic research with soul in mind.[2]

David H. Rosen
College Station, Texas

Acknowledgments

The shape and content of a book emerge slowly, much like the gradual finding of meaning in an analysis. I therefore begin by thanking David Rosen, who was convinced that I would be able to write something even before I had conceived of a topic. With a quiet persuasiveness on points of difference that made him difficult to resist, he has been a responsive and thoughtful companion at all stages of the journey toward completion of the manuscript. My profound thanks also go to Carolyn Grant Fay, without whose vision and generosity the Fay Lecture series would not exist at all. The lectures offer an invaluable opportunity for authors to write in depth on a subject that touches them and also brings therapists, students, and other interested individuals closer to Jungian ideas expressed in different ways in a wide range of cultural contexts.

A number of friends and colleagues have offered encouragement and support during fallow periods and have diligently studied drafts of the chapters in this book, commenting promptly and constructively. To them I owe a debt of gratitude. In particular, I offer my thanks to Richard Carvalho, Warren Colman, Catherine Crowther, Richard Mizen, and Christopher Perry. Pramila Bennett, administrative editor of the *Journal of Analytical Psychology,* offered me her editing skills and guidance on the mysteries of computer technology, permitting all the dots and commas to find themselves in the right places. Finally, I am grateful to my patients, who kindly agreed to permit me to publish accounts of some aspects of their analyses.

The Therapeutic Relationship

Introduction

When I was asked to give the Fay Lectures in April 2006, the initial excitement and anxiety generated in me not only an emotional energy that was a stimulus to action—to put pen to paper—but also an uncertainty about what topic to select. After a little time, the anxiety abated, and a clearer sense of purpose emerged. I wanted to study in depth a subject that continually inspires and tests me in my day-to-day clinical work with my patients. This is the subject of the transference in the analytic relationship, its meaning and value as an analytic concept, its significance for Jungian analysts today, and its uses and misuses with our patients. Of course, of central relevance, too, is the question of the extent to which working in the transference within the analytic process actually has the potential to help our patients recover from painful experiences so that they may learn to understand themselves better and ultimately to individuate creatively.

Consider first the following, short Aesop fable: "Every one of us carries two packs, one in front and one behind. The one in front is full of other people's faults, while the one behind is full of our own flaws. Because we cannot see our shortcomings, we imagine ourselves to be perfect—but we are all too quick to see the faults of others."[1]

This seems to me to be a startlingly clear and evocative example of transference; we project those aspects of ourselves we do not like—the pack at the back—onto others so that they may carry something that belongs to us until such time as we are ready to integrate it for ourselves.

In choosing to write about the concepts of transference and countertransference I was aware of the danger of putting new wine in old bottles since there have probably been more words written on the subject from a wide variety of perspectives than on any other subject within the domain of depth psychology. Surprisingly, today it remains as "hot" a topic for dispute as it was when Jung and Freud debated it almost a century ago. The forces to remain the foot soldiers in the battles of our parents are always strong.[2]

My expectation in writing this book is to stimulate in the reader an interest in the complex concepts of transference and countertransference and how they operate in practice. Jung is often quoted as uninterested in working with the transference, but although, unlike Freud, he did not leave us extended clinical case studies illustrating how he worked with transference material, his writings and clinical vignettes show evidence of a profound intellectual and emotional interest in the phenomenon from personal and archetypal perspectives developed, often at some cost, out of his own clinical practice.

I hope to evolve a more contemporary Jungian approach to working with transference and countertransference that takes account of Jung's views while acknowledging, too, that his thinking in this area was marred by significant flaws. Jung was inconsistent in his views on transference probably because of his vulnerability to the transference projections of his patients, in particular, the erotic transference. His discovery of the centrality of the analyst's personality and of the role of countertransference in the analytic relationship is evidence of his brilliant intuitions and pioneering thinking, but he lacked a coherent method and clinical technique for working with transference. What is more, his ambivalence and mercurial attitude toward matters of method could be seen to leave those eager to advance their skills in this area floundering and confused.

My personal background undoubtedly plays a significant role in shaping my approach to the subject of transference and countertransference. I trained at the Society of Analytical Psychology (SAP) in London, founded in 1946 by Michael Fordham. Together with the Jung Institute in San Francisco, the SAP was the first professional institute, after the analytical psychology clubs, established specifically to train budding analytical psychologists. Working closely with psychoanalysts in London, Fordham tried to integrate valuable ideas from psychoanalysis, including the transference process, into Jungian psychology. Because of this, the cultural climate in which I trained has inevitably biased my thinking in favor of a central role for transference in my clinical practice. In these chapters the reader will find references to some fine papers written by both psychoanalysts and analytical psychologists. However, integrating psychoanalysis with Jungian ideas can be hazardous since Jung and Freud had fundamentally different ideas about the nature of the unconscious. This will become clearer in chapter 1. Mindful of the possible biases in my own thinking while preparing my book, I recalled Jung's statement about his own writing: "Not everything I bring forth is written out of my head, but much of it comes from the heart also, a fact I would beg the gracious reader not to overlook if, following up the intellectual line of thought, he comes upon certain lacunae that have not been properly filled in."[3]

Our definitions of the concepts of transference and countertransference and the focus of contemporary debates have evolved over time. We now have a wealth of theory and understanding about development from infancy onward, as well as rich clinical experience and relevant knowledge from other disciplines such as neuroscience and attachment theory. Thus, it would not be unreasonable to expect that the effects of transference projections from the patient onto the analyst and ways to work with them in the analytic relationship should be well understood by now.

The movement over time from seeing a phenomenon as a pathological process—an impediment to analysis—to viewing it as a normal part of all conscious and unconscious interactions is nowhere more evident than in discussions of transference and countertransference. I imagine that it would be difficult to find a Jungian analyst around the world who would now dispute the inevitability of transference projections making themselves felt within the analytic relationship and their significant role in the service of individuation. However, writing about these complex concepts today raises the crucial question of whether we are actually thinking, talking, and writing about the same thing. In order to creatively explore our views and differences on an issue, we need to be clear about what we mean. In addition, while we may use concepts comfortably, it is often more difficult to describe what we are doing in the consulting room. Problems of definition and of differences in emphasis, context, and culture can all influence the way in which interest in modern concepts evolves, thereby affecting analytic discourse and leading (sometimes awkwardly) to a confusion of dialects rather than to a creative space in which we can genuinely acknowledge differences and air disagreements.

Ideas about transference and countertransference are predicated not only on our views about the nature of the psyche and the development of mental functioning but also on our beliefs about the role of the analytic relationship and the aims of analysis. This raises the question of the relative significance of transference and countertransference within the network of concepts that influence analysts' practices, recognizing, of course, that some of these may not be fully conscious and thus are likely to be difficult to verbalize. It is my impression that analysts have diverse views of their aims and of what is therapeutic, which are affected partly by their affiliations with analytic institutes and key individuals within them and partly by social factors, clinical experience, and their own personalities.

We are brought together as analytical psychologists by two central beliefs: one in the power of the unconscious as altogether greater than the ego's capacity to comprehend it, and one in the value of the self as an organizing and unifying center of the psyche—an archetypal impulse to bring together and mediate the tensions between opposites. Analysis seeks access to the unconscious and the self in all of its aspects but likely privileges different "sites of therapeutic action,"[4] which leads to different methods of making sense of psychological experience with patients. Some analytical psychologists would assert that working in the transference, this specific way of being with individuals and coming to understand them, provides the most meaningful access to the unknown parts of the self and the development of identity. These analysts privilege the *process* of the analytic relationship over its content and prefer patients to use the couch to facilitate the process. Samuels refers to this method as the *interactional dialectic*.[5] Here, the emphasis in analysis is more on "relating" than "creating," though both are inherently psychological capacities.

Other Jungians privilege the objective psyche and rely more extensively on dreams, associations, active imagination, and amplification to locate its unconscious contents. In doing so they collaborate more consciously with patients to allow different aspects of the psyche to come into better alignment with each other. Samuels refers to such a method as the *classical-symbolic-synthetic*. Here, the *contents* and the potential creativity of the psyche as they emerge within the analytic relationship take precedence over the process. The transference and countertransference are less significant. These distinctions set the scene for what can be considered a somewhat problematic legacy that Jung has left us in relation to the concepts of transference and countertransference and their usefulness in clinical practice.

By extending outside the consulting room, our beliefs affect how we think, write, and teach. Institutionally, they determine the aims of each training curriculum, the syllabus for trainees, and whether the course is more academic or clinical in emphasis.[6] Jung claimed to want no disciples, yet the emergence of different clusters of beliefs advocated by key individuals has continued to create tensions about differences between various societies around the world—what Eisold has called "a continuum from Jungian orthodoxy to psychoanalytic collaboration."[7]

In the first chapter I present an overview of the theoretical and clinical development of the concept of transference in analytical psychology from Jung to the present day. This review illustrates the way in which Jung's complex relationship with Freud, which eventually led to a rift between them, left Jung deeply ambivalent about the significance of transference as a "site of therapeutic action." I use extracts from the marvelous Freud/Jung letters as my case material. Jung's ambivalence remains deeply felt in the Jungian community today and seems to me to leave analysts in clinical practice with some real dilemmas about how to understand and work with transference within the analytic relationship.

In chapter 2 I examine several of the key clinical controversies over transference and the way in which they have evolved into diverse approaches to methods of working with patients. Using clinical examples, I explore in particular the relevance of Jung's emphasis on the analyst's personality and what this actually means in practice. I make a central distinction between what I call "working in" the transference and "working with" transference.

Chapter 3 is called "Countertransference and Imagination." Here I link the process of imagination with analysts' use of their countertransference affects in the presence of their patients and suggest that countertransference is a special form of active imagination.

Jung's metaphor for the development of the transference, the *Rosarium Philosophorum*, emerged from his profound interest in alchemy and was expressed in a series of woodcuts dating from 1550. Chapter 4 describes this powerful metaphor and discusses the relevance of the *Rosarium* for clinicians in practice today. I put forward my own concept of *the transference matrix* as a contemporary model that honors Jung's central beliefs in the significance of the symbolic capacity but takes greater account of contemporary research findings in the fields of infant development, neuroscience, and emergence theory.

My final chapter has the provocative title "Transference for Life: Keeping the Patient in Mind." Working with the transferences of our patients can be life enhancing for some, but, if approached too dogmatically or mechanically, it can become a life sentence. Clearly the former is desirable, and in my experience our patients may need an analyst who is flexible when it comes to working with the transference if it is to be truly life enhancing. As I have already mentioned, Jung's method of working with transference material leaves something to be desired. Thus, in this last chapter I pull together some of central themes in order to evolve what I hope will be for the reader a meaningful method that combines some of Jung's heartfelt ideas with contemporary models of practice.

Inevitably, in a volume such as this, there will be some omissions. Erotic, psychotic, and negative transferences merit their own chapters, but these topics are not addressed specifically in this book.

Poets express emotions so much more elegantly than analysts. So, to end my introduction, I invite the reader to enter into the evocative and unconscious aspects of relating in two poems. The first, written by Emily Dickinson beautifully illustrates in vivo what could be thought of as an analytic relationship in harmony.[8] The second, an early poem by Robert Graves,[9] shows how difficulties in communicating can easily lead to misunderstanding and confusion:

I heard as if I had no Ear
    Until a Vital Word
    Came all the way from Life to me
    And then I knew I heard.

I saw, as if my Eye were on
    Another, til a Thing
    And now I know 'twas Light, because
    It fitted them, came in.

I dwelt, as if Myself were out,
    My Body but within
    Until a Might detected me
    And set my kernel in.

And Spirit turned unto the Dust
    "Old Friend, thou knowest me."
    And Time went out to tell the News
    And met Eternity.

EMILY DICKINSON

In Broken Images

He is quick, thinking in clear images;
    I am slow, thinking in broken images.

He becomes dull, trusting to his clear images;
    I become sharp, mistrusting my broken images.

Trusting his images, he assumes their relevance;
    Mistrusting my images, I question their relevance.

Assuming their relevance, he assumes the fact;
    Questioning their relevance, I question the fact.

When the fact fails him, he questions his senses;
  When the fact fails me, I approve my senses.

He continues quick and dull in his clear images;
  I continue slow and sharp in my broken images.

He is in a new confusion of his understanding;
  I am in a new understanding of my confusion.

ROBERT GRAVES

CHAPTER 1

Jung's Ambivalence about Transference

THE LEGACY FOR ANALYTICAL PSYCHOLOGISTS

The more acute the experience,
the less articulate its expression.

— Harold Pinter

In this chapter I explore the evolution of the concept of transference in analytical psychology from Jung to the present day. This review illustrates the way in which Jung's complex relationship with Freud led to an eventual rift between them and left Jung deeply ambivalent about the significance of transference as a site of therapeutic action. This ambivalence remains deeply felt in the Jungian community today and leaves those of us who work as practicing analysts with some real dilemmas as to how to understand and work with transference within the analytic relationship.

I have been struck by the lack of clarity with which authors discuss their personal views about transference, so much so that it is difficult to know whether authors are actually talking about the same phenom-enon. Victoria Hamilton uses Freud's term, the *analyst's preconscious,* to explore variations in psychoanalysts' preconscious beliefs and prac-tice: "It is in the area between avowed theoretical orientation—'I am a Freudian,' 'I am a Jungian,' on the one hand, and therapeutic actions in the 'here-and-now' exchanges of the clinical situation on the other that analysts reveal the muddled overlaps and uncomfortable coexistence of parts of belief systems."[1]

Hamilton's interest in the inner workings of the analyst's mind highlights the value of investigating and clarifying the organizing principles of different depth psychologies so that we can learn more about the significance and emphasis that different analysts invest in concepts (in this case, transference and countertransference) and how these manifest themselves in clinical practice. This is one of the tasks that I have set for myself in writing this book.

Theory, Pluralism, and Transference

A work that considers the evolution of theory and its effects on contemporary practice needs some preliminary thoughts about the nature of theory in analytical psychology and more particularly in transference and countertransference. The cumulative wisdom of our profession is embodied in our theory, and, by taking account of both the observed and the observer, analytical psychology has probably outgrown its initial classification as a "pure" natural science in favor of an approach more familiar to the social sciences.[2]

Frosh highlights how the central interest of analytical psychology and psychoanalysis—the unconscious—means that theory can never be completely objective: "If there is always unconscious activity, then one can never stand outside the system in order to observe its operations in a perfectly 'objective' way."[3] Forrester believes that, rather than debating whether analysis is a science, we should ask what kind of discipline it is. In his view, it is a stable discipline that produces knowledge, "an observational, naturalistic science of human beings, coping with complexity and variety."[4] Parsons, a psychoanalyst, highlights the subjective nature of our theory: "Psychoanalysis uniquely combines the scientific and the personal. . . . Its scientific nature is embedded in its personal nature: it is scientific *only in so far* as it is personal as well."[5]

Theory making, then, is a natural activity that can advance the knowledge of our profession. Pluralism does not uphold a one-world view but instead values equally a range of alternatives that can encompass conflict and compromise. Implicitly it acknowledges a role for subjectivity. But pluralism itself is complex. Samuels defines pluralism as an "attitude to conflict that tries to reconcile differences without imposing a false resolution on them or losing sight of the unique value of each position."[6]

This is the public face of theory. However, our "transference onto the concept of transference" reveals a darker personal face that can all too easily become the trigger for heated criticism and emotional conflict among colleagues. For example, those who work extensively in the transference are considered by others to have lost the essence of their Jungian identity to the psychoanalysts. On the other hand, those who downplay the transference by seeing it as a distortion of analysis are often seen as clinging blindly to Jung's ideas about the archetypes in the face of new evidence or overlooking significant aspects of the transference that demand attention.

So, a pluralist ideal may be all very well in theory but much more difficult in practice since theory making carries so much investment of feeling. Moreover, it is often difficult to separate the theories we believe in from our allegiances to their original proponents, be they valued or disdained internal or external figures.

For some authors pluralism has real dangers. Knox believes that "If the scientific paradigm is discarded altogether, pluralism can slide too easily into a post-modern multiplicity of theoretical narratives which have no connection with the growing body of empirical research in other disciplines about the way the mind takes in and organizes information."[7] She is convinced that we must draw on theory from elsewhere, especially theory about cognitive and developmental capacities that have been empirically verified in other disciplines.

Hogenson,[8] however, quoting Kitcher,[9] is aware of the dangers of turning toward other disciplines: "Once a creative investigator in one discipline becomes dependent on the insights of another science, he or she is always vulnerable to the vicissitudes and changes taking place in that science."

Stevens, like Knox, is rather skeptical about pluralism: "My position is that there exists a place for pluralism and contextualization but that Jungian psychology will destroy itself if it does not recognize certain basic principles, which are not 'beliefs' or 'fictions' but hypotheses which have passed certain empirical tests."[10] Hamilton, moreover, believes that pluralism is an ideal we rarely live up to: "Psychoanalysis has developed into a conglomerate of monistic systems that compete with one another, each advancing itself as the most comprehensive explanation of human pathology and development."[11] People seem, then, to aspire to pluralism, but it can seem gray in comparison to more black-and-white theories. Hamilton's point resonates with not only some of the present-day debates among Jungian analysts but also those between Freudian and Kleinian psychoanalysts in the United Kingdom.

Definitions of Transference

Various authors have defined *transference* in apparently similar but actually subtly different ways. All of them seem to agree that transference is an unconscious form of projection from the patient onto the analyst and a universal phenomenon. In the Tavistock lectures, Jung referred to transference as follows:

> The term transference is the translation of the German word *Übertragung*. Literally, *Übertragung* means *to carry something over from one place to another*. . . . The psychological process of transference is a specific form of the more general process of projection . . . that carries over subjective contents of any kind into the object. (my italics)[12]

Jung's emphasis here is a broad one on "subjective contents of any kind" and could encompass both personal and archetypal aspects.

Freud at first considered transference to be a block to progress—a form of resistance: "Transference in the analytic treatment invariably appears to us in the first instance as the strongest weapon of the resistance, and we may conclude that the intensity and persistence of the transference are an effect and an expression of resistance."[13] He introduced the concept of "transference neurosis," the pressure to repeat in the present repressed material from the past instead of remembering it.[14] Implicit in Freud's view is the inevitability that transference projections will make themselves felt within the analytic relationship between patient and analyst:

> The decisive part of the work is achieved by creating in the patient's relation to the doctor—in the "transference"—new editions of old conflicts; in these, the patient would like to behave in the same way he did in the past, while we, by summoning up every available mental force (in the patient), compel him to come to a fresh decision. Thus the transference becomes the battlefield on which all the mutually struggling forces should meet one another.[15]

Blum, a contemporary Freudian psychoanalyst, maintains that transference is actually "a return of the repressed," one in which memories that have been repressed in an unconscious fantasy constellation emerge into the analytic present.[16] Blum points out that transference is not literally a replay of the patient's early object relationships but more of a compromise formation, an unconscious fantasy that includes various components, including real experience, as well as self- and object representations, defenses, and superego factors. From this we can conclude that it tends to be the representations and fantasies about internal objects that are projected onto the analyst and are analyzed. Following Freud, Blum's strong emphasis on the repressed unconscious may be contrasted with Jung's greater interest in the projected contents of an unrepressed unconscious, what he called the *collective unconscious.* I return to this later in the chapter.

Fordham's definition of transference is more specific: "an unspecified number of *(unconscious)* perceptions of the analyst by the patient, caused by the projection of *split-off, or unintegrated parts of the patient onto or into the analyst*" (my italics).[17] He uses two words here, "onto" and "into," and although he does not differentiate between them, they seem to imply that the nature and power of the projective processes can be different. "Onto" conveys something less powerfully projected and introjected by the analyst, who seems in the traditional way to act more neutrally and thus be available to deal with patients' projections. "Into" is suggestive of a more forceful projective identification that invades the analyst, who will be affected, like it or not.

Fordham also writes about the "split-off or unintegrated" parts of the patient, showing his interest in trying to link Jungian and Kleinian ideas when developing his pioneering theory of the self and its development in infancy and childhood. These two terms (split-off and unintegrated) actually have rather different meanings.[18] *Splitting* was a term used by Melanie Klein and her followers to describe the primitive defense mechanism that people employ to preserve good experiences and evacuate the bad and intolerable so that they cannot contaminate each other. This was the earliest process by which internal objects were formed. Klein has been criticized for developing a model of "normal" functioning by using clinical data from her analysis of ill and damaged children. Fordham reserves the term *splitting* for disintegrative experiences that are pathological and threaten to overwhelm the infant or adult. He preferred instead the idea of deintegration and reintegration to describe the dynamic process whereby the primary self reaches out toward objects and internalizes experience.[19] His phrase "unintegrated parts of the patient" suggests that he is referring to the "not-yet-known" rather than the pathological or defensive. After all, splitting is necessary only when this process is significantly interfered with.

Jung's Ambivalence about Transference

One has only to survey Jung's writings on transference to discover a variety of points of view. To his followers, Jung left a confusing legacy about his thoughts and feelings about transference, which may contribute added heat to the intensity of debate today. For authors who wish to find evidence in Jung for their personal beliefs about transference, this ambiguity permits ample opportunity for extensive "narrative smoothing."[20] We would do well to remember that Jung's ideas about transference emerged in the context of the kinds of patients he was seeing at the time. These were often people in the second half of life who were visiting Switzerland from abroad for short periods of time, during which they would also most likely attend some of his lectures and seminars.

Steinberg and Fordham have written chronological accounts of Jung's developing ideas about transference, which spanned more than thirty-five years.[21] Over the years, Jung was often contradictory in his views, sometimes even within the same paper. Authors develop and change their ideas (hopefully with humility), and Jung's modifications of viewpoint may be understood in the context of the era in which they were written, the debates of the day, and those to whom they were presented. Susan Rowland, in her book *Jung as a Writer*, is kind to Jung on this matter. She maintains that Jung's heartfelt belief in the creativity of the psyche extended to his style of writing: "For Jung, a piece of writing was only truly valid if it retained a trace of spontaneity that he believed to be integral to psychic functioning."[22]

However, the question remains, Why are Jung's writings on transference so ambiguous? Steinberg contends that it is the only area in his writings where such major contradictions may be observed because Jung was hurt and angry with Freud for not sufficiently valuing his ideas.[23] Steinberg is also of the opinion that Jung had emotional difficulties with his patients' transferences, particularly the erotic, and their effect on him: "This may have led him to play down the significance of the personal component of the transference and try to find other means of treating his patients."[24]

Jung's writings do indeed support Steinberg's view: "I am personally always glad when there is only a mild transference or when it is practically unnoticeable. Far less claim is then made upon one as a person, and one can be satisfied with other therapeutically effective factors."[25] Jung's treatment of Sabina Spielrein (his first analytic patient) provides compelling evidence of his struggles with the transference. In a recently discovered letter of Jung's first approach to Freud after Sabina Spielrein's discharge from the Bürgholzli, Jung writes the following: "During treatment the patient had the misfortune to fall in love with me. . . . In view of this situation her mother therefore wishes, if the worst comes to the worst, to place her elsewhere for treatment, *with which I am naturally in agreement.*"[26]

Jung's hurt and anger are expressed in one of his personal letters to Spielrein: "I have eliminated from my heart all the bitterness against you which it still harboured. To be sure this bitterness did not come from your work . . . but from earlier, from all the inner anguish I experienced because of you—and which you experienced because of me."[27]

Henderson, who was one of Jung's analysands, reminisces about Jung's methods and recalls that, when patients developed too powerful transferences onto Jung, he would refer them to Toni Wolff "to be reminded," as Jung put it, "of their specific problems and the practical solutions which came from a flexible use of the reductive method of analysis."[28]

Fordham is more generous about Jung's inconsistencies in terms of his attitude toward the transference, finding a greater consistency of evidence as to why, at crucial points, Jung held the views he did if the reader shows perseverance.[29] Using the Tavistock lectures as an example, he helpfully points out that Jung may have taken a negative view of transference out of annoyance that his audience distracted him from his devoted study of archetypal dream material to ask about his views on transference.

As my case material for this lecture, I would like to use extracts from the letters that passed between Jung and Freud in the spring and summer of 1909.[30] These letters provide a fascinating and moving account not only of Jung's early struggles to manage the transference—most particularly the erotic transference with Sabina Spielrein—but also of Freud's attitude toward his friend's difficulties. In 1909 Jung was Freud's golden boy and beyond reproach, and Freud's transference to Jung seems to have blinded him unhelpfully to the complicated relationship between Jung and Spielrein. At times Freud supported Jung almost unconditionally rather than exploring with him more robustly the transference and countertransference difficulties in his analysis of Spielrein, with which he clearly needed help.

Here are the extracts I have chosen:

MARCH 7, 1909: JUNG TO FREUD
A complex is playing Old Harry with me: a woman patient, whom years ago I pulled out of a very sticky neurosis with

unstinting effort, has violated my confidence and my friendship in the most mortifying way imaginable. She has kicked up a vile scandal solely because I denied myself the pleasure of giving her a child. I have always acted the gentleman towards her, but before the bar of my rather too sensitive conscience I nevertheless don't feel clean, and that is what hurts the most because my intentions were always honourable. But you know how it is—the devil can use even the best of things for the fabrication of filth. Meanwhile I have learnt an unspeakable amount of marital wisdom, for until now I had a totally inadequate idea of my polygamous components despite all self-analysis. Now I know where and how the devil can be laid by the heels. These painful yet extremely salutary insights have churned me up hellishly inside, but for that very reason, I hope, have secured me moral qualities, which will be of the greatest advantage to me in later life. The relationship with my wife has gained enormously in assurance and depth.[31]

MARCH 9, 1909: FREUD TO JUNG

I too have had news of the woman patient through whom you became acquainted with the neurotic gratitude of the spurned. When Muthmann came to see me, he spoke of a lady who had introduced herself to him as your mistress, thinking he would be duly impressed by your having retained so much freedom. But we both presumed that the situation was quite different and that the only possible explanation was a neurosis in his informant. To be slandered and scorched by the love with which we operate—such are the perils of our trade, which we are certainly not going to abandon on their account. *Navigare necesse est, vivere non necesse* [it is necessary to sail; it is not necessary to survive].[32]

MARCH 11, 1909: JUNG TO FREUD

Your kind words have relieved and comforted me. You may rest assured, not only now but for the future, that nothing Fliess-like is going to happen. I have experienced so much of that sort of thing; it has taught me to do the contrary at all times. Except for moments of infatuation my affection is lasting and reliable. It's just that for the past fortnight the devil has been tormenting me in the shape of neurotic ingratitude. But I shall not be unfaithful to psychoanalysis on that account. On the contrary I am learning how to do better in the future.[33]

JUNE 4, 1909: JUNG TO FREUD

Spielrein is the person I wrote to you about. . . . Since I knew from experience that she would immediately relapse if I withdrew my support, I prolonged the relationship over the years and in the end found myself morally obliged, as it were, to devote a large measure of friendship to her, until I saw that an unintended wheel had started turning, whereupon I finally broke with her. She was, of course, systematically planning my seduction, which I considered inopportune. Now she is seeking revenge. Lately she has been spreading a rumour that I shall soon get a divorce from my wife and marry a certain girl student, which has thrown not a few of my colleagues into a flutter. What she is now planning is unknown to me. Nothing good, I suspect, unless perhaps you are imposed upon to act as a go-between. I need hardly say that I have made a clean break. . . . On top of that, naturally, an amiable complex had to throw an outsize monkey-wrench into the works. . . . Now of course the whole bag of tricks lies there quite clearly before my eyes.[34]

JUNE 7, 1909: FREUD TO JUNG

Such experiences, though painful, are necessary and hard to avoid. Without them we cannot really know life and what we are dealing with. I myself have never been taken in quite so badly, but I have come very close to it a number of times and had a narrow escape. I believe that only grim necessities weighing on my work, and the fact that I was ten years older than yourself when I came to psychoanalysis, have saved me from similar experiences. But no lasting harm is done.

They help us to develop the thick skin we need to dominate "countertransference," which is after all a permanent problem for us; they teach us to displace our own affects to best advantage. They are a blessing in disguise.[35]

I had to tell myself that if a friend or colleague of mine had been in the same difficult situation I would have written in the same vein. I had to tell myself this because my father complex kept on insinuating that you would not take it as you did but would give me a dressing down more or less disguised in the mantle of brotherly love. For actually it is too stupid that I of all people, your son and heir, should squander your heritage so heedlessly, as though I had known nothing of all these things.[36]

Fräulein Spielrein has admitted in her second letter that her business has to do with you; apart from that, she has not disclosed her intentions. My reply was ever so wise and penetrating; I made it appear as though the most tenuous of clues had enabled me Sherlock Holmes–like to guess the situation (which of course was none too difficult after your communications) and suggested a more appropriate procedure, something endopsychic as it were. Whether it will be effective, I don't know. But now I must entreat you, don't go too far in the direction of contrition and reaction. Remember Lassalle's fine sentence about the chemist whose test tube had cracked: "with a slight frown over the resistance of matter, he gets on with his work." In view of the kind of matter we work with, it will never be possible to avoid little laboratory explosions. Maybe we didn't slant the test tube enough, or we heated it too quickly. In this way we learn what part of the danger lies in the matter and what part in our way of handling it.[37]

I have good news to report of my Spielrein affair. I took
too black a view of things. . . . The day before yesterday she
[Spielrein] turned up at my house here and had a very decent
talk with me, during which it transpired that the rumour
buzzing about me does not emanate from her at all. My ideas
of reference, understandable enough in the circumstances,
attributed the rumour to her, but I wish to retract this
forthwith. Furthermore, she has freed herself from the
transference in the best and nicest way and has suffered no
relapse (apart from a paroxysm of weeping after the separation).
Her intention to come to you was not aimed at any intrigue
but only at paving the way for a talk with me. . . . Caught in my
delusion that I was the victim of the sexual wiles of my patient, I
wrote to her mother that I was not the gratifier of her daughter's
sexual desires but merely her doctor, and that she should free
me from her. In view of the fact that the patient had shortly
before been my friend and enjoyed my full confidence, my
action was a piece of knavery which I very reluctantly confess to
you as my father. . . . I ask your pardon many times for it was my
stupidity that drew you into this imbroglio.[38]

Don't find fault with yourself for drawing me into it; it was not
your doing, but hers. And the matter has ended in a manner
satisfactory to all.[39]

These extracts make compelling reading and, from my point of view,
shed some light on the ambivalence in Jung's writings on transference.
Embarking on his first piece of work as an analyst with Spielrein, Jung
states clearly that a complex of his own, presumably his vulnerability to erotic feelings for women, "threw an outsize monkey-wrench
into the works" and was dramatically exposed. When Jung found
himself in difficulty with his patient, reaching out to Freud for help
was an ethically sensible decision. Although the letters suggest that
Jung worked through what we might today call a countertransfer-

ence enactment and that he transformed it, with Freud's help, from anger at his patient into a more reflective and rueful fellow feeling, it is understandable that this experience may have made him wary of too much personal involvement with his patients. The evidence suggests that the mutual idealization that existed between Freud and Jung at this time may have blinded both of them for a while to the process of reflection necessary to understand the transference dynamics. Not long after this incident, this idealization inevitably turned into disappointment and disenchantment and ultimately ended their relationship, pushing Jung further away from an interest in transference because it remained of central importance to Freud.

I cannot end this commentary on the Freud/Jung letters without saying something about Freud's striking remarks to Jung about how the analyst should deal with countertransference affects (I return to this in chapter 3). Freud begins by highlighting the need for the analyst to "dominate countertransference," which entails acquiring a thick skin so the analyst is not taken over by feelings and desires; later, however, he presents a remarkably modern description of countertransference. Using Lassalle's analogy about a chemist trying to understand why his test tube has suddenly cracked, he tells Jung to expect inevitable "small explosions" in analysis and explains that these may be a means of learning from experience, whether the explosion occurred because of something intrinsic in the relationship between patient and analyst or because the analyst had not managed the situation very well.

Jung's Views about Transference

Despite many inconsistencies, Jung has made significant theoretical contributions to the study of transference, emphasizing as he did both its purposive and therapeutic aspects and the significance of the analyst's "real" personality.

In lecture 5 of the Tavistock lectures, Jung outlines what he considers to be four necessary stages of working with transference.[40] I have summarized his stages in my own words:

1. to help patients come to acknowledge and value their subjective images, personal figures, inner objects, and so on that are projected onto the analyst

2. when these are worked through, to help patients distinguish between the personal projections and those that are impersonal or archetypal

3. to help patients differentiate the personal relationship with the analyst from impersonal factors and to help them consciously realize that they are not just personal but carry an impersonal, archetypal value that can take them forward

4. to help the patient realize that "the treasure" lies within, not outside, and that it is "no longer in an object on which he depends"—what Jung called the "objectivation of impersonal images," an essential part of the process of individuation

These stages contain very complex ideas about the nature and role of the transference. Furthermore, as stand-alone statements, they do not help analytical psychologists-in-training grasp *how* to work with transference material. Questions arise as to how to distinguish between personal and archetypal transference projections; whether the process evolves in neat stages like this; and how to work with defenses against the processes Jung outlines in the preceding four stages.

A major difficulty is that Jung did not tell us how to carry out these steps, perhaps because he was of the view that technique devalued the individual nature of analysis. Moreover, Jung did not extend his theory to include the role of infancy and the development of the self from birth. He took what might be seen as a more adult and sophisticated approach to transference.

Whatever the clinical limitations of these four stages, embedded within them lie Jung's central beliefs about transference:

a) Jung is generally in agreement with Freud in supporting analysis of the infantile transference:

His [the analyst's] highest ambition must consist only in educating his patients to become independent personalities, and in freeing them from their unconscious bondage to infantile limitations. *He must therefore analyse the transference,* a task left untouched by the priest.[41]

b) In contrast to Freud, who was interested in causality, Jung stresses the purposive value of the transference. In an early letter to Dr. Löy, he writes:

As long as we look at life only retrospectively, as is the case in the psychoanalytic writings of the Viennese school, we shall never do justice to these persons [neurotic] and never bring them the longed-for deliverance. . . . But the impulse which drives the others out of their conservative father-relationship is by no means an infantile wish for subordination; *it is a powerful urge to develop their own personality,* and the struggle for this is for them an imperative duty.[42]

Using Aristotle's ideas, Jung made a helpful distinction between two kinds of causality, what he called *causa efficiens* and *causa finalis* to clarify his preferred emphasis on the purposive aspects of the psyche.[43] *Causa efficiens* seeks reasons for happenings, whereas *causa finalis* asks "to what purpose is it happening?" Unlike Freud, Jung believed that helping his patients connect their past experiences with the present would not only help them learn how these could cause difficulties in the present but also help them move forward. Understanding the roots of patients' emotional difficulties and the inevitable regression involved can, Jung believed, facilitate contact with archetypal experience. In his view, patients project parts of themselves not yet known into the analyst in order to learn about them.

c) Jung is more comfortable with a synthetic method.

Jung criticized Freud's heavy emphasis on infancy and the reductive method as insufficiently valuing the present and potential meaning to the individual of unconscious, spontaneous productions such as dream images and symptoms. His preference (though not exclusively) for working toward a synthetic method embodied his view of the purposive character of the unconscious and its symbol-making capacity:

We know that it is possible to interpret the fantasy-contents of the instincts either as signs, as self-portraits of the instincts, i.e. reductively; or as symbols, as is the spiritual meaning of the natural instinct.[44]

d) Jung differentiated between personal and archetypal transference.

His stages of the progress of analysis distinguish between images that emerge in the transference from patients' personal experience and those that emanate later from impersonal structures of the psyche. The way Jung writes can easily give the impression that he wanted the personal out of the way, moving with more interest to archetypal, transpersonal transferences, but his acknowledgment of the significance of both is observable in his writing:

The personal projections must be dissolved; and they can be dissolved through conscious realization. But the impersonal projections cannot be destroyed because they belong to the structural elements of the psyche. They are not relics of a past which has to be outgrown; they are on the contrary purposive and compensatory functions of the utmost importance.[45]

The archetypal transference has two specific characteristics. First of all, archetypal transference projections are more clearly parts of the self that are not yet integrated; second, when they appear during the work, their contents suggest that they are a forward-looking communication that prepares the psyche for individuation. Archetypal transference material does not demand interpretation but rather needs some kind of acknowledgement in the analysis. Some Jungian analysts would amplify material emerging from archetypal transference content with reference to myths and stories.

e) Jung understood the archetypal nature of the transference process intuitively and intellectually. This is expressed clearly throughout *The Psychology of the Transference* and in his account of the transference phenomena using illustrations from the *Rosarium Philosophorum* and holds up well to this day:

> Once the transference has appeared, the doctor must accept it as part of the treatment and try to understand it, otherwise it will be just another piece of neurotic stupidity. The transference itself is a perfectly natural phenomenon which does not by any means happen only in the consulting room—it can be seen everywhere and may lead to all sorts of nonsense, like all unrecognized projections. Medical treatment of the transference gives the patient a priceless opportunity to withdraw his projections, to make good his losses, and to integrate his personality.[46]

f) Jung believed that the transference should and could be resolved: "The detachment of the patients' projections from the doctor is desirable for both parties and, if successful, may be counted as a positive result."[47]

Like Jung, Henderson believed that transference projections can be worked through, leaving a "symbolic friendship" with the analyst, especially later in the analysis, when personal transferences have been worked through.[48]

In the absence of a personal analyst, Jung turned to studies of history, anthropology, and mythology to amplify his intuitions about the unconscious psyche and the relationship between patient and analyst. Some view his detailed unfolding of the analytic relationship through the alchemical text of the *Rosarium Philosophorum* (see chapter 4) as his main work. Not to everyone's taste, the *Rosarium Philosophorum* is difficult to understand and can leave students who are eager to advance their clinical practice lost instead in its abstract metaphors.

However, Jung's parallels between the individual's striving for inner unity and the alchemists' search for the lapis, the philosopher's stone, are truly original and highlight the way in which Jung's usual use of the term *transference* refers to the analytic relationship as a whole, in contrast to some of the more specific definitions quoted earlier. I refer the reader to Perry's and Kirsch's skilled expositions of the woodcut series for their relevance for day-to-day work in the consulting room.[49]

Post-Jungian Contributions to Transference

One of the most methodologically significant post-Jungian contributions to the theory and clinical use of transference is Mary Williams's work on the relationship between the personal and the collective unconscious.[50] She maintains that Jung did not separate these concepts in an arbitrary manner when treating patients, although his writings can give this impression. She points out that the personal and collective unconscious in image-making and pattern-making activities are always interdependent:

> Nothing in the personal experience needs to be repressed unless the ego feels threatened by its archetypal power. The archetypal activity which forms the individual's myth is dependent on material supplied by the personal unconscious ... the conceptual split, though necessary for purposes of exposition, is considered to be undesirable in practice.[51]

Much of the contemporary Jungian writing on transference has a greater clinical emphasis, developing Jung's ideas and making them more relevant and accessible to therapists in practice. As one of the first analysts to explore and question some of Jung's key beliefs about transference, Michael Fordham gave frequent and helpful case illustrations in his extensive writings as a way of bringing Jung's ideas into the consulting room in a vivid way.[52] Fordham mistrusted Jung's reliance on the analyst's personality (see chapter 2) because he believed that it could easily lead to idealizations by patients and acting out by analysts. In his view, the manner in which analysts manage the transference is crucial. Analytical psychologists who turn away from the word *technique* as diminishing the personal dimension in each analysis risk avoiding a more careful scrutiny of the interactive process. Fordham's research into Jung's synthetic method reveal his pessimism and doubt that an educative approach can deal helpfully with patients' transferences—in particular, the more intense, sometimes delusional ones that emerge when working with borderline and severely narcissistically damaged patients in analysis.

Following Jung's distinction between the personal and the archetypal transference and taking into account his early personal difficulties managing certain transference projections, Plaut believes that analysts cannot avoid being affected by archetypal transferences who will inevitably "incarnate" the internal figure projected:[53] "I should still consider that in selected cases there is a place for the analyst to incarnate an archetypal image, to allow for the 'primitive wonderworld.'"[54] The danger for the analyst lies in identifying with this figure and either not recognizing it or sensing it and resisting.

Other authors have built psychological bridges between Jung's central ideas and modern-day practice. Davidson illustrates how a good analysis can be thought of as a lived-through active imagination and emphasizes the need for the analyst to receive transference projections from patients with an attitude that is favorable to an internal process of active imagination.[55] More recently, Cambray has drawn on the literature on subjectivity and intersubjectivity to reformulate Jung's method of amplification as an internal process that occurs as part of analysts' countertransference responses to their patients. His article helps to bridge the division between those analysts who uphold and those who dismiss the value of amplification in their work, stressing that "to most fully employ amplifications, recognition of our felt engagements with the images and stories that come to mind is essential."[56] References to other recent post-Jungian and psychoanalytic contributions to the study of transference and countertransference can be found later in the book.

Despite these more recent attempts by authors such as Williams, Plaut, Davidson, and Cambray to link inventively some of Jung's original ideas with contemporary practice, I maintain that Jung's ideas about transference have indeed left a confusing legacy for those of us who have trained as Jungian analysts. Using extracts from the Freud-Jung letters, I have illustrated Jung's personal struggle to process powerful transference projections and their complementary countertransference affects in his treatment of Sabina Spielrein. This experience may have left him wary of future, powerful personal transferences with his patients. As Jung and Freud gradually became estranged, Freud's growing interest in transference may well have contributed to Jung's diversion elsewhere to develop his research. However, these two reasons alone are insufficient to explain the emotionally tense disagreements about the significance of transference that are palpable in the Jungian world today.

For this we must turn to several problematic conceptual muddles. There is probably general agreement among all Jungian analysts that transference happens and that it is a natural, archetypal process with a purposive function. Patients unconsciously project as-yet-unknown aspects of their psyches into their analysts in order to discover through the analyst more about themselves. However, particular differences begin to emerge when we ask the following questions: How do we work with our patients' transference projections, and how central do we consider them to be as a site of therapeutic action?

It has clearly been difficult for analysts to live with Jung's ambivalence about transference. Some have turned for greater clarity and certainty to psychoanalysis, where the strong interest in transference among Freudians and Kleinians has fleshed out the concept, as well as its applications in practice. Adhering more closely to Jung's core beliefs, others choose, like Jung, to work with personal transferences only when they have to, retaining a stronger interest in ways to facilitate the development of a symbolic capacity with their patients. Behind these compromise solutions lies a veritable Gordian knot of theoretical confusions that have clinical implications for working with the transference.

Jung's Use of the Word Transference

From my reading of Jung's deliberations on transference, it seems to me that, although his texts several contain consistent definitions (e.g., his idea of *Übertragung*, the carrying of something from one place to another), Jung primarily used the term *transference* too broadly and vaguely. He did not want to limit the meaning of transference to the projections of parental imagos and instead preferred a definition that would encompass not only archetypal and personal projections in the present but also one that could preserve the role for the symbolic child.[57] Too broad a definition may cause the concept of transference to lose its meaning altogether and become a description of the analytic relationship as a whole rather than of the specific aspects discussed earlier.

Jung's interest in alchemy and the symbolism of the *Rosarium Philosophorum* were intended as metaphors not only for the process of individuation but also for the stages of development in the analytic relationship, what Jung calls the *transference*.[58] This is a confusing conflation of process and outcome. In analysis, Jung contrasts the initial experience of *participation mystique* (process), what we would today call *projective identification*, in which personal transference projections during the analysis may lead to a state of unconscious identity between patient and analyst, with the *coniunctio (outcome)*, a higher-order psychological mechanism[59] that is "always the product of a process or the goal of endeavour."[60] In other words, it is the hoped-for outcome of an analysis (which psychoanalysts might refer to as the *development of a well-functioning internal couple*) that emerges later in the analysis, when the patient becomes more conscious. In my experience, the transference emerges in different ways with different patients during an analysis. Transference, it should be remembered, is an unconscious process, an inevitable part of any analysis, stronger sometimes, quieter at others; occasionally it is directed clearly onto the analyst and at other times onto other people in the patient's life. I am not sure that it evolves in clear stages, as Jung suggests, and I believe that we mix up process and outcome if we consider the term as a description of the analytic relationship as a whole.

Different Conceptions of the Nature of the Unconscious

Freud and Jung held different views about the nature of the unconscious. Freud considered transference to be "new editions of old conflicts," as described earlier.[61] Blum's description of the transference as "the return of the repressed" implies that transference is essentially both repetitive and regressive and provides little room for the emergence of anything new.[62] Freud was interested mainly in *the repressed unconscious*. Although he acknowledged that the repressed does not cover everything that is unconscious, for the most part his methods and those of the post-Freudians concentrate on analyzing the resistance and defenses that emerge in analysis as a result of ideas that have already come into consciousness. These have usually emerged in childhood but, because of their threatening nature, have been repressed: "The essence of the process of repression lies in preventing it from becoming conscious. When this happens, we say of the idea that it is in a state of being 'unconscious.'"[63] Jung himself and Jungians today are generally more interested in *the unrepressed unconscious*, better known as *the collective unconscious*. In Williams's words, "Jung ceded the personal unconscious to Freud, and the collective unconscious and the archetypes became his province."[64] The collective unconscious as we know it is ultimately unknowable; Jolande Jacobi expresses this with elegance: "the unfalsified voice of nature, beyond the judgment of the conscious mind and uninfluenced by the environment.[65]

In contrast to Freud's concept of repression, visualized as a form of horizontal splitting, Jung conceived of the normal psyche as essentially dissociated, implying a vertical rather than a horizontal division. Freud's repressed unconscious is different from Jung's idea of subpersonalities, the fragmentary personalities that he came to call *complexes*. Jung's view is that dissociation rather than repression is the main mechanism for keeping mental contents out of consciousness but allowing space for the "not yet known," the unrepressed, to emerge.[66] Dissociation is not necessarily pathological, and the spontaneous expressions of the psyche, with their motivations and affects, are not necessarily defensive. Freud's system was too closed for Jung, but more important, in terms of my thesis, their different conceptualizations of the nature of the unconscious suggest different states of mind in which analysts are likely to attend to their patients' transference projections.

Overdetermined Distinctions between the Personal and the Archetypal Transference

I have already referred to Mary Williams's clear elucidation of the indivisibility of the personal and the collective unconscious. These cannot really be separated, and to do so can lead to the danger of idealizing both the archetypal and its contents. In the introduction to his book *Jung and the New Age,* David Tacey gives examples of this. For instance, the New Age movement, especially in the United States, has unhelpfully appropriated Jung as one of its spiritual leaders: "turning the spiritual realm into a commodity, packaging ancient wisdoms, indigenous cosmologies and spiritual psychologies in order to satisfy our spiritual longing."[67]

Tacey believes this New Age consumerist mode actually fails to meet our spiritual needs since artificial quick fixes do not provide the authenticity the human spirit longs for. I believe we devalue the role of the personal at our peril, and keeping the personal and the archetypal connected at all times permits a more integrated and ultimately valuable approach to working with transference.

Differences in the Elucidation of Meaning

Most Jungians are interested less in the sources of unconscious material than in their meaning. However, different methods of elucidating meaning in analysis are likely to have major implications for an approach to the transference. The unconscious has a natural tendency to express itself in symbolic language, and these symbols are informative for both patient and analyst. Some analysts prefer, like Jung, to take a more educative and synthetic approach to symbols when they emerge in sessions or in dreams, supported by Jung's largely *intrapsychic* model of the psyche. Here the analyst is looking for unconscious signs and symbols that can be elucidated with the patient. Other analysts, however, believe that the unconscious emerges more naturally through the analytic relationship in the transference. The presence of the archetypal and its symbols emerges out of the conscious and unconscious relationship, implying an *interpersonal* approach to the analytic relationship and a greater significance for the subtleties of personal interactions. The first approach is a more receptive technique in that it trusts in the natural energy and creative capacity of the self. The second places more weight on the therapeutic alliance and the analyst's interventions and searches for meaning in the analytic relationship.

In this chapter I have conveyed some of the reasons for Jung's ambivalence with regard to transference and explained why he has left us with such a complicated theoretical and clinical legacy. Managing difference is never easy. Indeed, we all strive to achieve it but encounter numerous failures along the way. Jung's approach to transference is confusing because of his early, intense personal experiences with his patients. In light of Pinter's words at the beginning of the chapter, I believe we can forgive Jung for the times when he is less than articulate on the subject.

It is probably true that, whichever transference direction we ourselves have taken, we are likely to have missed out on certain views had we chosen another route. We must try to resist dividing analytical psychology into two transference camps—the developmental and the classical. It is essential to keep both alive in the consulting room, even if they are likely to make somewhat uncomfortable bedfellows at times. As analysts and patients, we need the capacity both to *relate* and to *create* in order to harness the archetypal energy necessary for the process of individuation. We fail our patients and their very different individual needs if we cannot encompass both approaches. In my opinion, this is a necessity for analytical psychologists who are working with the wide variety of patients that present in our private practices and our hospital settings today.

CHAPTER 2

Working "in" and Working "with" the Transference:

EMBRACING DIVERSE APPROACHES

A cake cannot be made of nothing but currants.

— James Strachey

In this chapter I move on from Jung's ambivalence about transference and its legacy for analytical psychologists in practice today. Here I discuss some of the key clinical controversies over transference facing us today and explain how they have evolved into observable, diverse approaches that we can employ in working with transference in the consulting room.

Michael Fordham's address to members of the Society of Analytical Psychology (SAP), London, at its annual general meeting in July 1954 highlighted the central role of transference in debates among its members:

A new sign of activity within the Society has been the continued interest in the transference, 'round which is circulating some of the conflicts within the society. If my reading of these conflicts is correct, they turn on the questions, not of the existence of transference phenomena, but upon the desirability, or otherwise of interpreting some of them in personal terms, and on the ways of handling and reacting to transpersonal contents.[1]

The minutes of this meeting reflect the work of a small group of SAP members more than fifty years ago to engage creatively but stringently with the subject of transference and to determine whether and how to interpret it. Although the central tenet of Fordham's address holds true today, the areas of difference and dispute have shifted in focus. While the existence of transference and countertransference affects in the analytic relationship may no longer be disputed in the Jungian community, our ways of handling transference communications and our own countertransference responses seem to me to vary enormously.

Areas of Controversy

There exist today some major areas of controversy over the significance of transference, the weight to be given to it in the therapeutic process, and the nuances of taking up transference projections with our patients:

a) whether, as Jung believed, transference is a *natural phenomenon* that is common to all relationships or a *special manifestation* of the particular relationship that develops between patient and analyst that can even be induced.[2] In my view, it is certainly universal but appears in analysis in a particular form facilitated by the stance of the analyst, who is trained to pick it up and work with what Sandler et al. call this "specific illusion which develops in regard to the other person."[3]

b) whether transference is a *unidirectional* phenomenon or rather *multidirectional* in its essence. A unidirectional meaning suggests that transference refers mainly to Freud's idea of repetition and regression in the patient, which are caused by a past problem (see chapter 1). For example, patients may come with strong negative feelings (developed in childhood) about authority figures; these feelings may be related to their personal authoritarian father and lived out in the transference with their analyst. A multidirectional approach is altogether more Jungian in that it allows for the emergence of something new and creative in the analysis. It is not just a present repetition of past complexes. Thus, although transference can emerge in analysis as a present repetition of an aspect of a relationship with someone from the past (i.e., an externalization of an internal object), it can also reflect a present mood that is unconscious to the patient or indeed a new, present transference relationship.

c) whether transference should be given only a *limited place in the therapeutic process,* in contrast to the view that it is *crucial to analyze everything that occurs in the transference.* Going even further, some analysts in the United Kingdom believe that nontransference interpretations, such as making links with the patient's past or considering the meaning of an image or a symbol, constitute an intellectual avoidance of the hot spots in the here-and-now of a session. For these analysts, who are often Kleinian in orientation, transference interpretations are held to be the only ones likely to lead to any significant psychic change.

d) whether particular aspects of the analysis *do or do not constitute transference.* Jung stated clearly that analysis can be transforming for both analyst and patient, surely implying that analysis is more than transference alone. What is more, Jung talked about "the real relationship" between patient and analyst, marking a significant role for the analyst's personality and distinguishing this from the transference relationship. Psychoanalysts tend to refer to this as "the therapeutic alliance." It seems that some analysts consider the analytic relationship to be a transference relationship in its entirety, whereas others firmly uphold the need for a distinction between the transference relationship and the real relationship.

e) whether transference is, as Freud implied, a resistance or cul-de-sac or, as Jung preferred, a means of opening up new possibilities via the projection of what is as yet unknown by the patient into the analyst.[4] Samuels finds a place for both by making the helpful distinction between the personal "ghosts" of the past, which must be carefully exorcized before growth is possible, and the more valuable archetypal "ancestors," who carry the potential for symbols to emerge into consciousness, so vital for the growth and development of identity.[5]

Case Vignette

Here is a short account of a dream told by a patient to one of my supervisees. It serves as an illustration of the potential for diverse approaches to working with the transference in the consulting room:

The patient, Bob, is a twenty-five-year-old man who has been seeing a male analyst four times a week. After two years in analysis, Bob brings the following dream to a session shortly before the summer break:

> The patient is visiting a house where there is some kind of party, and someone is cooking beef burgers that are still raw in the middle. The analyst is present in the dream. Other people are given books as presents, and Bob is given a book on architecture. Bob is disappointed. The book does not reflect his interests sufficiently well. It is black and white and too rigid. He tries to exchange the book for something else. In another scene of the dream, Bob arrives at his analyst's house and rings the doorbell. The analyst does not answer immediately but comes to the door after Bob rings a second time.

Most of you would agree that, at first glance, this dream involves transference. Bob has had a dream in which his analyst appears not once but twice. The analyst is first of all present at the party in a somewhat neutral way, and in the second scene of the dream, the analyst fails to respond at first to Bob.

More controversial, however, might be the way in which different analysts think and feel about this dream. Some might assume that the dream was *all* about transference (i.e., the analysis is still raw in the middle, and more work needs to be done). Perhaps the analyst is not yet able to detect something the patient is trying to tell him; thus, Bob has to press his buttons pretty hard to be noticed. Is the analyst in the dream being too black and white in his approach to Bob? Some analysts might feel personally challenged by Bob's dream, alerted in consequence to the need to attend to their own complexes. What have they been missing, and why?

Then there are questions about the context of the dream. Is this one of a series of dreams or a "big" dream? Is this Bob's usual way of bringing in a dream, or is there something different about it? Could it have been told with the unconscious intention of testing the analyst?

Some colleagues might be more cautious about the transference and instead focus on the alchemical imagery of cooking or ponder whether the reference to the book on architecture suggests that Bob needs to develop something other than his thinking ability. Different analysts are thus likely to approach Bob's dream in a variety of ways. Presumably we would first ask Bob for his associations, thoughts, and feelings about the dream. We could choose a specific image such as "raw beef burgers" or "books on architecture" and ask him directly to play with these images rather than picking up the transference immediately.

What is immediately and strikingly obvious in this dream is the wide range of potential meanings. Of course, the patient's thoughts and feelings about the dream will be central as it is *his* dream, but I have presented this vignette to make a point. I want to make here a central distinction between what I refer to in this chapter as *working in* the transference and *working with the transference.* Working *in* the transference is a given in all analyses. We cannot avoid it. It is there whether we like it or not. In contrast, as analysts we are constantly faced with challenging choices when it comes to working *with* the transference. My questions about the preceding dream show that we have choices about whether to interpret the dream's transference content to our patients, and, if so, how and when to do so. Analysts' discussions about these choices are intriguing and can trigger emotional conflicts among colleagues. Some of you may be familiar with comments such as these: "How could she work in that way?" "He doesn't understand the transference!" "She is just using the transference mechanically, not authentically."

New Contexts for Understanding Transference

In 1935 Jung made this remarkable observation: "Emotions are contagious, because they are deeply rooted in the sympathetic system. . . . any process of an emotional kind immediately arouses a similar process in others . . . Even if the doctor is entirely detached from the emotional contents of the patient, the very fact that the patient has emotions has an effect on him."[6] In the light of recent compelling evidence in the fields of mind-brain research and infant development, Jung's remarks seem quite modern since he intuits that, whether we like it or not, analysts are likely to be unconsciously affected by their patients. Thus, using my terminology, we are always likely to be working *in* the transference.[7]

It is now well established that the development of the brain and the development of mind are significantly related and, further, that the development of a mind and the capacity to make meaning emerges through relationship. Nonverbal and unconscious interactive processes go on continuously in infancy and adulthood and therefore by implication within the transference-countertransference relationship. Implicit processing that is beyond awareness can be as important as that which is explicit, conscious, or verbal. Some excellent experimental and clinical research studies show the implications of damage to these implicit interactive processes.[8]

Schore describes the way in which the brain always organizes itself in the context of another person with another brain.[9] He stresses that affect regulation underlies and maintains the functioning of the individual. It in turn is affected nonverbally and unconsciously through relating. His findings have implications for both analytical psychology and psychoanalysis, which have tended until relatively recently to focus more heavily on the symbolic meaning of verbal communication. Schore's research supports the idea that nonverbal communication regulates mind and body in interpersonal relationships and by implication between patient and analyst:

Non-verbal transference-countertransference interactions that take place at preconscious-unconscious levels represent right hemisphere to right hemisphere communications of fast-acting, automatic, regulated and dysregulated emotional states between patient and therapist . . . In a growth-facilitating therapeutic context, meaning is not singularly discovered, but dyadically created.[10]

Pally is in agreement with Schore: "How the analyst feels, both 'in the body' and 'in the mind,' may be as important an indicator of what is going on in the patient as whatever the analyst is thinking. How the analyst communicates may be as important as what the analyst says."[11] The implications for analysts to find the capacity to access both their own subjective responses and rational thoughts are clear. Working from the premise that the nature of interactive processes is now seen as central to both infant development and the success of the analytic endeavor, Beebe and Lachmann use a dyadic-systems model to study the origins of relatedness and patterns of nonverbal communication in infancy and adulthood:[12] "A person is affected by his own behaviour (self-regulation) as well as by that of his partner (interactive regulation). Interactive regulation flows in both directions, on a moment-to-moment basis."[13]

Stern et al. capture the essence of these ideas with their phrase *implicit relational knowing,* the intersubjective unconscious experiences in analysis that are *moments of meeting,* new experiences that are just as important as interpretations in precipitating change in analysis.[14] The process of making implicit knowing conscious is not the same as accessing repressed material. What is significant is that these "moments of meeting" are new and that something is created intersubjectively that alters the analytic atmosphere.

Lyons-Ruth stresses that "these moments of meeting open the way to the elaboration of a more complex and coherent way of being together, with associated change in how relational possibilities are represented in each participant's implicit relational knowing."[15] These and other findings lend credible support to the value that analysts place on giving careful attention to the processes of transference and countertransference, as they are central to the recognition and facilitation of change.

They also confirm transference as an archetypal process. While patients project onto and into their analysts, both are in the psychological soup together—*in* the transference. In the context of the finding that subjectivity is an emergent and interactive process, Jungian theory stands up pretty well to the research tests of time. Jung's emphasis on both the mutuality of change in analysis and an indefinitely extended sphere of nonconsciousness is supported by the findings of neuroscience and infant development research. His concept of the transcendent function[16]—an individual's capacity to enable the rational and the irrational, the conscious and the unconscious to be compared and ultimately to come together—sits well with Stern's implicit relational knowing and the need for analysts to bring together what they sense and what they think in order to develop a capacity for both self-regulation and interactive sensitivity. The research findings also give us food for thought as to how we can educate potential analysts to fine-tune their subjective experiences with their patients and internalize a capacity to self-regulate and contain primitive experience. Tracking patients' affective states in relation to the analyst's is an essential component of the analytic attitude. How we may convert these into a meaningful language with which to talk to our patients remains controversial. Among depth psychologists, the specific disagreements about transference and countertransference have been reframed but not resolved. What we know now from the fields of infant research and cognitive neuroscience promises to help us better understand the precise mechanisms by which transference processes operate.

Two Central Transference Controversies

I now turn to a more detailed discussion of two central controversies to which I referred earlier. Each has the potential to cloud in a different way our attitudes toward the analytic relationship and the choices we face in how to work *with* our patients' unconscious transference projections and their effects on us.

TRANSFERENCE: THE TOTAL OR PARTIAL SITUATION?

The phrase "transference: the total situation" is the title of Betty Joseph's article on her idea that transference is the central framework for all analyses.[17] She follows Klein's ideas with regard to transference as "total situations transferred from the past into the present as well as emotion, defences and object relations."[18] In other words, it is not just transference onto the analyst that is significant and may be interpreted; rather, everything that patients bring to analysis gives clues about their immediate, unconscious anxieties aroused in the transference relationship. Joseph states, "My stress has been on the transference as a relationship in which something is all the time going on, but we know that this something is essentially based on the patient's past and the relationship with his internal objects or his belief about them and what they were like."[19]

Later Joseph summarizes her own position:

> Everything in the patient's psychic organization based on his early and habitual ways of functioning, his fantasies, impulses, defences and conflicts, will be lived out in some way in the transference. In addition, everything that the analyst is or says is likely to be responded to according to the patient's own psychic make-up, rather than the analyst's intentions and the meaning he gives to his interpretations.[20]

Joseph believes that the main site of therapeutic action lies within the transference relationship. It seems to me that the Kleinian attitude to transference, so influential in the Society of Analytical Psychology, of which I am a member, is predicated on the supreme significance of infantile, unconscious fantasies that are active in the here and now, all the time implicitly locating the infant-mother dyad as the main location of disturbance. Troubles start at this earliest point, and only if these hot spots become lived experience within the analysis and interpreted through the here and now of the transference can internal change become possible. Appropriate attempts to interpret past experience as significantly influencing the present are not excluded but downplayed as defensive on the part of patient or analyst and of lesser therapeutic value than here-and-now interventions.

This view has led to much difference of opinion among psychoanalysts. The ongoing debate between Blum and Fonagy, for instance, as to whether the here-and-now transference experience of self and other is the most important site of therapeutic action is mentioned in chapter 1.[21] Fonagy's distinctions between explicit and implicit memory leads him to question the usefulness to the analytic endeavor of the process of recovering childhood memories.[22] He agrees with Joseph: "Therapeutic work needs to focus on helping the individual identify regular patterns of behaviour based on childhood fantasy and experience, for which autobiographical memory can provide no explanation."[23] In his view the only way we can really know what goes on in a patient's mind is by studying the transference.

Blum challenges Fonagy's position: "We do not know our patients' character through transference alone and the analyst is not the only transference object . . . extra-transference interpretations involve extra-analytic transferences."[24] Blum values transference as one useful element for understanding our patients but believes it is no more reliable than others, such as dreams, symptoms, and certain behaviors. In a more emotional tone he criticizes analysts whose sole focus is on the transference:

> How does the patient feel when only transference is interpreted and other issues are ignored? All associations, interventions and reactions are forced into the Procrustean bed of transference. A strictly analytic transference focus is consistent with a narcissistic position of the analyst; he/she is not only a very important person but is considered the most important person in the patient's life. The patient identifies with the idealized analyst, and the narcissism of the analytic dyad is then gratified and promoted. This is especially problematic in a long analysis if real-life relationships have been devalued and cannot compare to the exceptional status and satisfactions.[25]

Blum overstates his case a bit, but his voice resonates among some analytical psychologists. Peters is of the opinion that transference develops naturally and should not be forced through premature or dogmatic transference interpretations by the analyst.[26] He believes that patients bring transferences onto figures other than the analyst, which, if worked with, do not preclude effective analysis. He agrees with Blum, warning analysts of the dangers of excessively incarnating the archetype of the infant-mother relationship, which leads them, in his view, to impatiently draw their patients' transferences toward them. Samuels also acknowledges the centrality of the transference but also advocates a significant role for the relational, intersubjective, nontransference aspects of the analytic relationship.[27]

Using detailed clinical case material, Astor contrasts the relationship between his internal psychoanalytic supervisor and his Jungian supervisor as they interact and are played out in the analysis of a female patient.[28] He maps out from within himself the controversy of the relative importance of the transference. His internal Jungian supervisor trusts in the organizing capacity of the self, values the manifest content of the patient's material, and finds a valid role for empathy and nontransference interpretations. In these terms, transference material is not necessarily always buried. Astor's internal psychoanalytic supervisor considers the task of analysis to be that of bringing unconscious fantasy into the open. The patients' communications always have unconscious meaning in the here and now of a session. Astor uses his empathy and intuition about his patient's feelings and state of mind to find the approach most helpful at any particular time.

In *Controversies in Analytical Psychology* (Withers 2003), Kast and Proner enter into a spirited debate about the relative significance of the transference.[29] Kast is clear about her view: "Facilitating the development of symbols is more important than the process of transference-countertransference itself. Symbols are not only vehicles for the individuation process but also refer to life history and future development ... They shape the emotions that are connected with complexes, archetypes and the real relationship."[30]

Proner disagrees, conceptualizing the analytic relationship as "analogous to an early mother-infant couple" and emphasizing the need for access to feelings and images associated with infantile parts of the psyche reworked with the analyst. He agrees with Joseph, who specifies transference as the central site of therapeutic action. Proner sees Kast's approach as "analysing the transference," whereas he himself works "in the transference," highlighting a methodologically significant difference between them. In Proner's view, "all material brought to the analytic session, whether verbal or nonverbal, whether dreams or free associations, communicates something about the ongoing inner relationship between the patient and the analyst."[31]

My own distinction is subtly different from Proner's, whose definition of working "in the transference" implies something deeper and more relational than Kast's emphasis on symbols per se. The distinction I make between "working in" and "working with" the transference avoids a potentially divisive split among Jungians. I maintain that we all work *in* the transference all of the time, but it is our personal choice as to what we work *with*—what we interpret to the patient— that leads to diverse approaches.

This discussion of transference as the total situation then highlights three central differences of opinion:

1. whether transference is theoretically the "fulcrum of analysis"[32]
2. whether everything the patient brings emanates only from the infantile parts of the psyche
3. the nature of the effect on the patient when the analyst takes up all communications in the here and now of the transference

I agree with Fonagy's statement that "the crucial component is the provision of a perspective or a frame for interpreting subjectivity that is beyond that which the patient has ready conscious access to apart from the analytic encounter."[33] This comes close to my concept of working *in* the transference. However, like Etchegoyen, I believe that "not everything is transference, but transference exists in everything, which is not the same thing."[34]

I work *in* the transference in that I am usually alert to its presence, and I also work *with* the transference; in other words, I actually interpret it and do so quite often. I agree that transference is the fulcrum of analysis since I hold that it is only when the relationship in the room is alive that real change is possible. However, I cannot agree that transference is "the total situation." If *all* interpretations are transference interpretations that have the aim of uncovering patients' complexes in relation to the analyst, this can become a particular kind of reductionism. As a result, patients risk learning "a method" from the analyst that limits their possibilities for creative play, in which symbols can find meaning and dreams herald new possibilities. With this comes an inherent danger that we listen *for* transference rather than listen *to* our patients. To return to Strachey's evocative quote about transference at the beginning of this chapter, "a cake cannot be made of nothing but currants."[35] A transference-only cake is a poor cake indeed and not one that I would like to serve up at my own analytic table or at that of my supervisees. My cake would be full of tasty ingredients and would be light and moist to eat. It would take a while to perfect the mix of ingredients, cooking time, and temperature, and, as those of you who are bakers know all too well, the excellence of the outcome can never be guaranteed.

Infantile transference is always there, and when it emerges from patients' earliest experiences, it is usually felt within the analytic relationship. If "received" in body and mind by the analyst, it can lead to an authentic experience from which meaning can be discovered. Frequent sessions and the use of the couch are likely to foster preverbal and intense transference projections, but the transference is not always infantile. If we view (and interpret) transference as emanating only from infancy, then we risk losing both the complexity and the temporality of the meaning of our patients' communications and the way the mind functions at different developmental stages.

2. THE ANALYST'S PERSONALITY

Jung was wholehearted in his view that the analyst's personality is central to the success of an analysis: "Every psychotherapist not only has his own method—he himself is that method . . . the great healing factor in psychotherapy is the doctor's personality."[36] He also stressed the equality of the analytic relationship, "in which the doctor, as a person, participates just as much as the patient. . . . We could say without too much exaggeration that a good half of every treatment that probes at all deeply consists in the doctor examining himself, for only what he can put right in himself can he hope to put right in the patient."[37]

The significance of both the analyst's personality and the equality of the relationship between patient and analyst is nowhere more evident than in Jung's now famous quotation:

> By no device can the treatment be anything but the product of mutual influence, in which the whole being of the doctor as well as that of his patient plays its part. In the treatment there is an encounter between two irrational factors, that is to say between two persons who are not fixed and determinable quantities but who bring with them, besides their more or less defined fields of consciousness, an indefinitely extended sphere of non-consciousness. Hence the personalities of doctor and patient are often infinitely more important for the outcome of the treatment than what the doctor says and thinks.[38]

Intuitively, it is difficult to disagree with Jung's impassioned words, but it is much more difficult to unpack what they actually mean in clinical practice. Obviously, the analyst's personality is significant since we all bring to the analytic situation the essential and unique characteristics of the people we have become. Jung is referring here to the way in which analysts use themselves when working with patients. His considerable emphasis on personality was in part his reaction to the much-caricatured Freudian emphasis on neutrality, abstinence, and anonymity, vestiges of the old medical model. Although the findings of neuroscience and infant research show that nonverbal, unconscious processes are going on all of the time, thereby influencing both patient and analyst, the personal analysis, training, and clinical experience of analysts put them in a better position to bring these interactions into consciousness. Because of this, I find it unhelpful to think about the relationship between patient and analyst as having the symmetry that Jung implies.

Analysts need the capacity to both hold back and move forward in the analytic relationship. Anonymity, abstinence, and neutrality are to my mind intrinsic constituents of a professional analytic and ethical attitude. We reveal only minimal information about our personal lives to our patients, leaving "space" for transference projections (*anonymity*).

We limit enactments and acting out *(abstinence)* and maintain a non-judgmental attitude *(neutrality)*. These contribute to the creation of a *vas bene clausum,* or containing space, in which relating can safely evolve.

We also need the capacity to move forward in the sense of making ourselves emotionally fully available to our patients. Receptiveness to projections and projective identifications is a vital component of the analytic attitude. I believe this is what Jung was talking about when he advocated a new theory for each patient[39] and what Fordham was encouraging by "not knowing beforehand,"[40] creating the potential for the emergence of new theories in each session. It is Bion's eschewing of memory and desire so that the analyst "increases his ability to exercise acts of faith."[41] This involves what I describe as the "self of the analyst." Schafer similarly states that analysts must subordinate their own personality in analytic work and refers to "a second self." He contends that it is artificial to separate this second self from the analyst's personality, for it is "a form that integrates one's own personality into the constraints required to develop an analytic situation."[42] I believe he is talking here about a considered way of using himself in the service of his patients.

Controversies about the role of the analyst's personality in the analytic relationship include debates about whether analysis is a real relationship and how much of themselves analysts should reveal to their patients. Although Greenson recommends that analysts constrain themselves from expressing genuine feelings to their patients, he frequently cites examples of situations in which he views such revelations as therapeutically beneficial.[43] Renik, too, challenges contemporary ideas about countertransference. He believes that since the analyst's subjectivity is inevitably transmitted to the patient, analysts might as well bring their views out into the open.[44] In my experience this can often be counterproductive. It is the analyst's self-knowledge that patients really need, what we might describe as a very subtle blend of competence and character.[45]

The range of views about how much analysts should give of themselves has been aired in a debate between Caper and Colman. Caper, a psychoanalyst, maintains that we always unconsciously wish to influence our patients rather than analyze them.[46] He considers this to be an aspect of the analyst's neurotic countertransference and asserts that it happens because analysts cannot hold back from freely offering themselves in the presence of obvious suffering. We must necessarily exclude "too many of the elements vital to any ordinary, natural human relationship."[47] Being too real, he states, leads to collusions with the patient, and even if this approach appears superficially therapeutic, it is not, in his view, analytic.

For Caper, the analyst's main role is to make transference interpretations:

> The real job of the real analyst is to identify and understand the meaning of both the transference and countertransference fantasies in terms of split-off parts of the patient's personality and to communicate this understanding to the patient. In this view, providing the patient with anything else, such as love, advice, guidance, or support for his self-esteem, is the analyst's acting in his countertransference and represents his resistance to analysis.[48]

Caper's view of analysts' technical stance and their attitude to the transference could be considered to be advocating more holding back by the analyst than moving forward. This analytic attitude privileges neutrality because, without it, patients will not discover their destructive impulses.

Colman claims that Caper's attitude risks inhibiting the development of a natural, unconscious process between patient and analyst. For Colman, "the therapeutic action of psychoanalysis occurs directly through the relationship between analyst and patient, rather than through the interpretation of its transference elements. Analysis is what is left after the interpretations have been forgotten."[49] Colman is saying that patients' experiences of their analysts as empathic and real can facilitate growth and do not necessarily constitute a longed-for defensive collusion. It is what comes from the "self" of the analyst that is important and will be felt unconsciously by the patient. Colman is not advocating countertransference enactments by telling patients what he feels in sessions; rather, he supports Jung's view that an uncontaminated transference is impossible and that interpretations are made in the analyst's mind out of this intensely personal relationship. Colman's stance gains support from recent research studies that demonstrate that what is felt in relationships can be more important than what is thought and that the way in which interpretations are conveyed may be more significant than their content.[50] The person of the analyst, however little is revealed, cannot be avoided in the analytic relationship, and it is this emotional contact that potentially facilitates change.

Case Vignette: Working in or with the Transference?

Michael, a man in his midthirties, was referred to me by a male colleague who had moved his practice out of London. A very intelligent man who does not find relationships easy, Michael is more comfortable living alone—"on the edges," as he puts it—in a world within his control and in which he neither feels threatened nor fears losing his identity. Wanting to continue his analysis, Michael came to meet me before finishing his analysis with my colleague but was uncertain about what it would be like to consult with a woman. He would not want to see me if I reminded him of his mother. I found myself alert to a possible negative transference dynamic should he decide to come to me for analysis. Seemingly this was not immediate, and we arranged to meet four times a week after he had finished seeing my colleague. The point here is that the transference was alive and kicking from our first meeting.

Michael, a doctor, has a position with important responsibilities in a large hospital. He works extremely long hours and sometimes has to make excruciatingly difficult triage decisions about patients who are hovering between life and death. He is gay, though he has not been in a relationship for several years. He indicated that when he gets involved, he becomes very sensitive and is easily hurt; thus, most of the time he believes that he is better off on his own. He lives in a world largely of his own making, quite isolated but also creative. He is taking an Open University course in psychology, plays the piano, and reads avidly. He is interested in Jung and has considered the possibility of training in the field.

The youngest of three children, Michael believes he was an accident. In childhood he was severely bullied by his older brother and remains angry with his parents for not protecting him more adequately. He characterizes his relationship with his mother as difficult and often combative, and he seems rather contemptuous of her. He loved his father very much and was devastated by his unexpected death a few years ago. He carries a strong internal picture of his father in retreat from his difficult mother, doing carpentry in his workshop. This, not surprisingly, has set the tone for the quality of the maternal transference in the analysis. Michael's unconscious identification with this capable father, who needed a place of his own away from the mother in order to be creative, has affected Michael's psychological development and led to an extremely cautious approach to intimate relationships and a belief that creativity is best practiced alone.

I like Michael. He is attractive, and there is a certain warmth about him, but it is not difficult to spot his extreme vulnerability. On the surface, he seems quite imaginative, but usually I experience him as talking to himself rather than to me. The analysis can be more like an imaginary retreat than a joint imaginative enterprise.[51] I find him hard to follow and often feel stupid in the face of his imaginings.

I had a strong intuition that I needed to warm him up somehow and that progress would be dependent on working *with* the transference, but this seemed a long way off and a delicate area to approach. Trial transference interpretations from me were met with resistance in the early days of his analysis. He told me that we did not have a relationship. Referring to his previous analysis, he could not understand how my colleague could talk as if a relationship existed between them: "How can you have a relationship with someone who does not say hello or goodbye?" He seemed to have moved to me as if from one impersonal relationship to another. He told me he had felt no grief about the loss of my colleague as his analyst, except for an experience of immediate shock when he was first told that the analysis would have to stop. I wondered about his need to defend himself against separation anxiety.

I was faced with a dilemma: Should I leave him alone to do it all himself, allowing myself to be "left at the edge" in the interest of Michael's greater emotional comfort? However, his creations often felt masturbatory—not creative at all—as if he left no room for me. In the grip of a strong countertransference feeling of exclusion early on, I decided to risk telling him when I felt lost in the face of his imaginings—when I believed he was talking to himself rather than to me. He understood. Then he told me that this was his idea of how analysis should proceed: He would come and talk, and the analyst would occasionally comment. I responded that this view allowed him to feel safe and unchallenged.

After the first summer break in the analysis, he returned and then announced that he wanted to discontinue our sessions. I felt surprised and shocked. He told me that he could not afford to come four times a week and wanted instead to buy an apartment. However, he did not want to stop altogether but merely wanted a gap in the analysis. Based on my hunch that separations were unconsciously very difficult for him, I made a transference interpretation, taking up his disappointment with me and his analysis and emphasizing the recent summer break.

He replied: "It is not you personally. It is the analysis."

I sat tight, interpreting the negative effect the break had had on him and his wish to punish me for having been away for so long. At the end of the session, I said that it would be a shame if he left his analysis so precipitously. I then felt as if I had been pulled into an unconscious rescue operation by going after a small boy who, after a tantrum, had locked himself in his bedroom. However, Michael continued to come to his sessions, although initially I did not know whether it was to please me or I had actually managed to contain something in the transference.

Gradually something began to shift, and I found myself moving from a silent recognition of the transference dynamics between us to a position in which I could begin to work *with* the transference more actively and actually interpret in the here and now of a session. I would like to describe part of a session with Michael during which I was able to track this movement:

He comes into my consulting room and tells me that he wants to take some time off work. He believes that he has been doing too much and that people are taking advantage of him. He wants to use the time to clear out his apartment. He thinks he might give up his office since he will be able to manage all of his administrative duties from the hospital.

He says that last night he was playing a Chopin nocturne on his piano at home. He now tells me for the first time that he has an electronic keyboard that has a recording device so that he can listen to what he has played. He states that this means he does not need a teacher. I comment that he is letting me know once again that he is perfectly capable of looking after himself and that he does not need a teacher/analyst.

Michael says that he is changing his views about analysis. He used to believe that it was just about coming to sessions and saying whatever was on his mind, while the analyst occasionally made impersonal interpretations. He is now beginning to realize that this is nonsense. Why has someone not told him it is also about relating? I assumed everyone thinks like me, he says, but the previous analyst said, "No, they don't."

I reply that he needed to discover this for himself. I feel pleased, as if we have moved into a different, more personal place in the analysis.

He then talks about a television program he watched last night. It was about Queen Elizabeth I. He tells me that, from her clothing, he now has in his mind an image of a piece of lace. He describes it to me, and I find myself forming my own image from his description. We begin very tentatively and for the first time in his analysis to play with his image. He is more spontaneous and open; I feel much more engaged.

I interpret this lace as having a dual function. It is a linking image in itself, and it is also making a connection between us at the moment.

He considers the lace to be very delicate and beautifully made. Then suddenly he says, "Now I want to throw it away. I thought of my mother, Elizabeth, Bet, Betty—that's her name."

I remark that his image of the beautiful piece of lace, which is allowing us to begin to play, seems quickly to have turned into a dangerous web that could entrap him. As a result, he has to get rid of it by discarding it and thereby pushing me away. I wonder whether I have gone too far too quickly. I also think about how, for Michael, a shared area can easily become a claustrophobic space from which he has to escape. I remember that Elizabeth I had an extremely strait-laced persona. However, she was at the same time capable of great passion, including a fury that led her to banish and even execute her lovers.

How might we think about this vignette? Michael is a patient with whom working *with* the transference has to be approached with caution and great care. He is a man who easily feels trapped or invaded and for whom intimacy is threatening. He has developed a hard yet brittle carapace of self-reliance, reminiscent of Kalsched's archetypal self-care system.[52] I wonder about his experience of early neglect as the third and unwanted child. In my view, premature transference interpretations would have driven him further away into his psychic retreat, his mental "workroom" where I was to be admitted only now and then. However, it is clear that we are also *in* the transference, living it during sessions, and I sometimes feel that I am an intruder who is trying to push in. I use my "reverie," a kind of meditative state of mind, to remain receptive to Michael's feelings and to name them and find a meaning that I hope will make sense to him.[53]

This is both an acknowledgement of the transference and a need to make sense of it in the hope that Michael will one day be able to develop his own capacity to reflect on his mental states. Reverie is not equivalent to a state of inactivity, however, though it may be disturbed when the analyst is preoccupied or under attack from patients. My countertransference experiences to keep my distance and proceed with caution at the beginning of the analysis have to be processed and transformed into an individual and helpful way of working *with* the transference. For Michael, the lace represents the emergence of a symbol of connectedness within him and between us. Something new has emerged from the analytic relationship into consciousness. We have affected each other. Because he is less cautious and defensive during this session, I have more freedom to enter his mental workroom to create something in a more playful way that includes interpreting the transference. The lace shows us that Michael is beginning to find the trust that permits him to play during the analysis, but it also warns me that his sensitivity—the maternal transference—is precarious and can easily be thrown away. I am holding in my mind both the tough and tender mindedness of Elizabeth I. Moreover, I have a hunch that, although these are different aspects of Michael that cannot as yet be integrated, they nonetheless infuse the atmosphere of the session with very different qualities of relating.

In closing, two of the main controversies over the role of transference within the analytic relationship discussed in this chapter—whether transference is truly the total situation and what role the analyst's personality plays—show the extent to which our attachment to specific ways of working can become intensely personal. Since as analysts we all need to become experts in the management of uncertainty, it is perhaps understandable that we long for a coherent theory that comprises a universal truth and a method of inquiry. It is also understandable that the back-and-forth pulls we feel between pluralism and unity, between learning from experience and learning from the hard sciences are nowhere more potent than in our theories of transference since these lie at the heart of the subjective, personal, and unique meeting of two selves that are trying to come together in an authentic way to make meaning. In my view and also borrowing liberally from Strachey,[54] some cakes will contain currants, others almonds, and yet others rich chocolate.

I return to Anthony Stevens's plea that Jungian psychology continue in its quest to "recognize certain basic principles, which are not 'beliefs' or fictions, but hypotheses which have passed certain empirical tests."[55] The research findings I have mentioned on the value of analysts' subjectivity as an emergent process uphold Jung's heartfelt views of the interactive nature of the analytic relationship, where the selves of patient and analyst consciously and unconsciously influence one another. The vignette of Michael's analysis brings this point to life. The research findings also support a central role for projective identification (in Jung's language, *participation mystique*) at the core of intersubjective relating. We cannot help but be affected by our patients, and, consequently, we ignore transference phenomena at our peril.

While definitions of transference can be teased out relatively straightforwardly, its use in the consulting room is much more complex and requires great sensitivity. Perhaps the point is that whatever the theory or belief system (about transference) we adhere to, we should practice it authentically. It is authenticity that our patients need and want from us, and, arguably, this is what can ultimately help them to know themselves better. Practicing authentically means acknowledging that we are always working *in* the transference even if we hold different views about its value and the various ways of interpreting it to our patients.

I work both *in* and *with* the transference. In the consulting room, the nature of the transference as a lived experience that involves both patient and analyst permits infantile states of mind to emerge and new mental states to be discovered. It is our readiness to move between the past and the present with our patients, the personal and the archetypal, the old and the new, and the defensive and the purposive that makes transference from a Jungian perspective a truly complex and multidirectional concept. Diverse approaches are inevitable and are to be embraced in the spirit of individual differences in practice that Jung left with us. In the words of Oscar Wilde, "the truth is rarely pure and never simple."

CHAPTER 3

Countertransference and Imagination

And, as imagination bodies forth
The forms of things unknown, the poet's pen
Turns them to shapes, and gives to airy nothing
A local habitation and a name.
Such tricks hath strong imagination
That, if it would but apprehend some joy,
It comprehends some bringer of that joy;
Or, in the night, imagining some fear,
How easy is a bush suppos'd a bear!

— Shakespeare, *A Midsummer's Night's Dream*

This short passage about imagination seems to me to conjure up marvelously the nature and process of countertransference. Imagination, one could say, permits glimpses of truth to be caught in analysis: in the patient, in the analyst, or between them. Such glimpses are embodied in those moments when something unconscious, as yet unknown, feels palpably present in the consulting room, ready to emerge into consciousness. It is then, as Shakespeare puts it, that the analyst's capability ("the poet's pen") is mobilized to productively use their countertransference affects in such a way as to transform for the patient "the forms of things unknown" into something with personal meaning that can touch the patient in both heart and mind. "Airy nothing" finds "a local habitation and a name."

The second part of the quotation alerts us to the mercurial aspects of imagination: Joy and fear, for example, can powerfully infect or distort our perceptions and render us unable to tell whether a good experience comes from inside or outside or whether what seems to be a threatening bear is really a benign bush. Our imaginings can inform us, but they can also be unreliable.

In a compelling review of the concept of imagination, British philosopher Mary Warnock arrives at what for her is the best definition: "It seems to be both plausible and convenient to give the name 'imagination' to what allows us to go beyond the barely sensory into the intellectual or thought-imbued territory of perception."[1] You now see why I call the third of my four chapters "Countertransference and Imagination," as these two terms are intrinsically linked. The analyst's empathic and creative use of countertransference is dependent on a well-developed capacity to imagine and to transform something that can be sensed into something with meaning that can be thought about and communicated. Countertransference is actually a special form of active imagination that creates a Jungian framework that can facilitate our understanding of the countertransference process and the ways in which analysts use it.[2]

First, however, I present an overview of several more general perspectives on countertransference.

Overview of the Concept of Countertransference

Countertransference, like transference, is a concept whose meaning has changed dramatically during the past century and especially the last fifty years. Originally, countertransference was always written with a hyphen, emphasizing that it emerged directly from the word *transference*. Alfred Plaut emphasized the need to differentiate *transference* from *countertransference:* "If counter-transference is given a special, positive place in theory and technique . . . it becomes a most useful indicator of the transference."[3] Nowadays the hyphen has disappeared in contemporary usage, and the concept has come to acquire a value in its own right with just as much equity as transference.

Freud formally introduced the term *counter-transference* in "The Future Prospects of Psycho-analytic Therapy," which he presented at the second International Nuremberg Congress in 1910.[4] In this address Freud described countertransference as the analyst's emotional response to stimuli that come from the patient and affect the doctor's unconscious. In his view, like transference, it was *an obstacle to progress in analysis* because it led him to advocate self-analysis as a way of helping analysts overcome their blind spots. A little earlier, in his letter to Jung in 1909, which I quote in chapter 1 (see pages 16–20), Freud had written less formally about the analyst's need for a strong, defensive, psychological and emotional skin in order to work in the field: "Such experiences [countertransference], though painful, are necessary and hard to avoid. *They help us to develop the thick skin we need and to dominate 'countertransference,'* which is after all a permanent problem for us; they teach us to displace our own affects to best advantage. They are a blessing in disguise."[5]

Later, in 1915, Freud clarified that he was not against analysts having feelings for their patients, but he did not view these as countertransference per se. He believed that analysts' personal conflicts and resistances could hinder them from acting as a mirror for their patients' material, including transference projections: "Our control over ourselves is not so complete that we may not suddenly one day go further than we had intended. In my opinion, therefore, we ought not to give up the neutrality towards the patient, which we have acquired through keeping the counter-transference in check."[6] Countertransference thus got in the way of what Freud was convinced was an essential position of neutrality. It is surprising that, despite his significant acknowledgement of its power over the analyst, he never returned to the theme in his writing.

Unlike Freud, the supreme and consistent value Jung placed on countertransference is implicit in much of his writing. He intuitively recognized the importance of the analyst's countertransference affects as part of the interactive, unconscious relating in analysis. Although he used the term only rarely, his commitment is evident: "All projections provoke counter-projections. . . . The counter-transference is then just as useful and meaningful, or as much of a hindrance, as the transference of the patient, according to whether or not it seeks to establish that better rapport which is essential for the realization of certain unconscious contents."[7] This is a remarkable statement from Jung because it evokes a paradox that continues to be debated today about the potential for the analyst's countertransference to foster both understanding and misunderstanding on the part of the patient. Perhaps for this reason, Jung was specific in his early recognition of the need for the analyst to be analyzed: "I even hold it to be an indispensable prerequisite that the psychoanalyst should first submit himself to the analytical process, as his personality is one of the main factors in the cure."[8]

Studies of the nature and the dynamic process of countertransference blossomed in the 1950s, especially among psychoanalysts, when authors realized that analysts' feelings and bodily sensations—their subjectivity—and their capacity to reflect on communications from patients were actually indispensable therapeutic tools and a significant pathway to the unconscious. Although woven into the fabric of Jung's fundamental conceptions about the nature of the analytic process, it was psychoanalysts such as Winnicott, Heimann, and Little and, later on, analytical psychologists such as Kraemer, Fordham, and Strauss who paved the way for the wealth of ideas about countertransference in the context of intersubjectivity and its related processes—projection, introjection, projective identification, containment, and enactment.[9] Jacobs made a most interesting cultural observation when he recognized that interest in the concept of countertransference was accelerated among analysts practicing in the 1950s, just after the Second World War, because they were so severely affected by their patients' war traumas.[10]

In 1950 Margaret Little realized the problems involved in precisely defining the concept of countertransference.[11] While essentially connoting a specific attitude or mechanism by means of which the analyst meets the patient's transference, the definition also had to include the analyst's own unresolved complexes and the effects these could have on their unconscious attitudes toward their patients and projections received from them as well. Little summarizes her view: "Countertransference is no more to be feared or avoided than is transference;

in fact, it cannot be avoided, it can only be looked out for, controlled to some extent, and used."[12] As a Jungian analyst with great respect for the archetypal and its capacity to hold us in its sway, I would be more skeptical than Little about analysts' capacity to control their counter-transference feelings.

Little's writing and Paula Heimann's papers finally established a central role for countertransference in analysis with all of its attend-ant dangers.[13] For Annie Reich, moreover, "countertransference is a necessary prerequisite of analysis. If it does not exist, the necessary talent and interest is [sic] lacking."[14] Ella Sharpe, too, not only con-firms its value but also challenges us in no uncertain terms to com-prehend its nature: "To say that the analyst will still have complexes, blind spots, limitations is only to say that he remains a human being. . . . We deceive ourselves if we think we have no counter-transference. It is its nature that matters."[15]

More Recent Conceptions of Countertransference

We now have far more detailed clinical descriptions of what goes on between analyst and patient, and it is clear that two related, open sys-tems are involved.[16] However, much like the term *transference, coun-tertransference* has come to acquire different meanings, and some would say that it is in danger of losing its meaning altogether. Today it is sometimes used by authors in a general sense to describe all of the feelings and thoughts that analysts have about their patients. More specifically, it retains a meaning that is more closely restricted to the feelings and thoughts arising in the analyst directly from patients' transferences. Etchegoyen's musical analogy puts it evocatively: "There is first canto, to which the contracanto responds."[17]

Fordham's definition complements the one expressed by Etchegoy-ens, and in my view it provides us with the most helpful perspective: "Transference and countertransference are essentially part and parcel of each other because both processes originate in the unconscious. The term [countertransference] will therefore be used here to cover the unconsciously motivated reactions in the analyst that the patient's transference evokes."[18]

In addition, Sandler, Dare, Holder, and Dreher have pointed out that the prefix "counter-" has two different meanings, adding a helpful coda to issues of definition.[19] "Counter-" conveys the notion of opposition (a reaction to the patient's transference), but it can also denote that something is complementary or in parallel, implying a counterpart. This distinction has formed the foundation for more contemporary writers to explicate the different kinds of countertransference reaction the analyst may experience.

Henry Racker published the first systematic study of countertransference. He viewed the analytic relationship as involving two individuals, each with both a healthy and a more neurotic aspect to their psyches; a personal past and present; and their own fantasies and relationship with reality.[20] His work focused on the analyst's inner experience and how it affects work in the transference. He distinguished first of all between *neurotic* countertransference affects, which develop when analysts become too identified with their own infantile feelings in relation to a patient, and second, what he called *true* countertransference affects. The latter fell into two types: first, the more comfortable, *concordant* responses, when analysts feel empathic with patients and even identify their own ego with that of the patient (Sandler's "parallel" meaning). The capacity for concordant countertransference affects is in turn related to the analyst's own experiences of "good enough handling by another when in a state of dependence."[21] The second type comprises the often more disturbing *complementary* reactions, when the analyst receives and identifies with the patient's internal objects (Sandler's "opposed" meaning). Grinberg extended the idea of complementary countertransference by putting forward the concept of *projective counteridentification,* which occurs when, in response to patients' projective identifications, analysts react (perhaps defensively) to their own countertransference responses.[22] In other words, when there are intense emotions in the room, these are not necessarily just the patient's projected inner world.

Among analytical psychologists, Fordham developed his ideas about countertransference from Jung's use of empathy, as well as *participation mystique,* a concept similar to projective identification.[23] Fordham distinguished between *illusory* and *syntonic* countertransference. Like Racker, he believed that analysts project their own material into their patients in a way that obscures their understanding of the patient. This unconscious process led to what he termed *illusory* countertransference. Fordham used the concept of *syntonic* countertransference to express the analysts' identifications with patients' inner objects, thereby encompassing in one term—*syntonic*—Racker's distinction between concordant and complementary reactions. The word *syntonic* comes from the field of telegraphy, where electrical instruments can be carefully and accurately tuned to each other's frequencies. This is the position of the analyst who is trying to tune in to signals coming from the patient's unconscious "transmitter." Later Fordham restricted his use of the term *countertransference* to the illusory because he believed that the necessary work on the concept of countertransference had been accomplished since analysts now realized they needed to scrutinize their subjective responses to their patients: "It is when the interactive systems become obstructed that a special label is needed, and, to my mind, it is then that the term countertransference is appropriate."[24] Fordham was convinced that the rest is "part of the interactional dialectic." Thus far, this idea has not proved particularly popular among subsequent writers, so Fordham may have been premature in his wish to restrict the term to the intrusion of aspects of the analyst's inner world.

Samuels maintains that there are two useful but different forms of countertransference.[25] The first he calls *reflective* countertransference, which may occur when analysts experience a feeling of depression or anxiety that is not their own but rather their patients' unconscious depression. It is the patient's depression that is reflected in the mood of the analyst. The second form, what Samuels calls *embodied* countertransference, is connected to an inner object of the patient. For example, the patient may have internalized an experience of a depressed mother and projected it onto the analyst. Both experiences are syntonic, but the first reflects an experience in the here and now between patient and analyst, whereas the second, embodied countertransference, implies the emergence into consciousness of a longer-term complex of the patient that affects the analyst's countertransference feelings.

Jungian authors have contributed significantly to the elaboration of the shadow aspects of countertransference. For instance, in describing a range of potentially dangerous countertransference enactments by the analyst, Jacoby focuses on money, power, erotic feelings, and the neurotic need for therapeutic success.[26] Additionally, Lambert warns of enactments in the countertransference when the analyst becomes caught up in talion law and unconsciously treats attack with counterattack when identified with the patient's hostile inner objects.[27] Guggenbühl-Craig and Groesbeck explain that analysts can become identified with the "healer" archetype, leaving their patients as the only "wounded" ones.[28] Furthermore, Stein shows that analysts can harm their patients if they overlook the dangers not only of the abuse of their power but also of seductive shamanism or an idealization of the unconscious.[29]

Countertransference, then, like transference, is actually a most complex phenomenon. Definitions have certainly moved on from Freud's narrow interpretation of countertransference as a block to progress, arriving at present-day views that it comprises all of the analyst's conscious and unconscious responses to patients—in other words, whatever the analyst thinks and feels is countertransference. Samuels refers to this latter perspective as "the countertransference revolution,"[30] a swing that definitely goes too far. Sandler, too, cautions against what he calls "wild countertransference analysis,"[31] and his words are echoed by Spillius: "Although I think the use of the ideas of projective identification and countertransference have greatly enriched our understanding of the analytic relationship, we also need to be aware of the dangers of placing too much emphasis on our own feelings instead of closely observing the patient."[32] I agree with both Sandler and Spillius. Such definitions render the term almost meaningless. What is evident from my own practice as analyst and supervisor is that countertransference, because it is essentially an unconscious process, inevitably provokes anxiety. Margaret Little makes a wise observation: "Unconscious countertransference is something which cannot be observed directly at first, but only in its effects."[33]

The art lies in learning to remain psychologically open to our patients' transference projections and in developing the capacity to appraise their meaning, including an acknowledgement of our own blind spots and complexes. With this in mind we may view countertransference as a joint creation between patient and analyst, implying as it does the significance of both the analyst's subjective responses and the projected aspects of the patient's inner world. Countertransference both influences the process and holds within it rich opportunities for its understanding. Analysts' professional and personal identities are inevitably involved in the process, and there is also a valid role for all analysts' associations, intuitions, images, and thoughts that are *not* countertransference but part of their general responses to their patients. What continues to be debated today is how this translates into individual methods of practice and whether analysts' reflections on countertransference affects are, with all of their attendant dangers, the central mutative activity in analysis.

Case Vignette: Syntonic or Neurotic Countertransference?

Sophie is a patient I have been working with four times a week for about four years. She is a rewarding patient who works hard in her sessions, brings dreams, and has an interest in her inner world. She has a highly competent exterior, expressed in a rather manic, overactive persona that frequently uses up nearly all of her ego resources to stave off a needier and more vulnerable child subpersonality. I feel she is always very careful of me, acutely watching all of my reactions to her as a way of keeping me at a safe distance but under scrutiny. Usually late for sessions, Sophie arrives in a near-permanent state of exhaustion that I interpret as her unconscious demand to be soothed and calmed without too much challenge or penetration. Sophie's father was a self-centered lawyer who was a bully. Her mother was intensely anxious and took rather poor care of her child. Sophie is in her thirties and has been unhappily married for ten years to a businessman, with whom she frequently becomes frustrated and angry. They have two young children.

I present two sessions to illustrate the emergence of my countertransference affects and their effect on the analytic relationship at that time.

As Sophie arrives, I am preoccupied with the unexpected disappearance of my much-loved cat. During the first part of the session, aware of my intense anxiety and having catastrophe fantasies that my cat has been eaten by a fox or run over, I close my eyes in an attempt to calm down and compose myself so that I can give Sophie my full attention. I am not entirely sure, but I think that, when closing my eyes, I may have dropped off to sleep for a moment or two. Sophie uses the couch, so in order to look at me she has to turn her head toward me.

Sophie has arrived feeling very depressed. Two months ago her horse died, and she misses her. She loved and rode this horse for many years, although the animal was sometimes difficult; it would become intensely jealous and was prone to lash out at other horses and people. Because Sophie's family generally planned their weekends around the horse and riding activities, their routine has been disturbed since the animal's death. Sophie tells me that, this past weekend, she and her husband visited friends, one of whom tried to cheer her up by asking her to choose the colors for their new house, something Sophie usually enjoys. Sophie, a school governor, tells me that she also attended a depressing meeting over the weekend. She thinks she should resign from her position since she has not been attending meetings regularly for some time and feels she is not pulling her weight.

Suddenly I hear Sophie say, "I think I am sending you to sleep?"

I reply, rather instinctively, "No, I don't think so" (wondering whether I am defensive and immediately feeling guilty in case I did indeed fall asleep).

I rally after this exchange and manage to give Sophie my full attention. After the session, I feel very uncomfortable. My own preoccupations, what I considered to be my neurotic countertransference, have prevented me from being fully available to Sophie. I wonder what effect this will have on her. I am relieved when my cat appears at suppertime, having been quietly sleeping unnoticed in an upstairs closet.

The next morning Sophie comes to her session with a dream:

She is in a school auditorium, and she and her husband are sitting in different places. There is a registration desk, and someone is calling people's names. She is waiting for her own name to be called. Then she is outside the school, and the senior teacher is welcoming new parents and taking little notice of Sophie and her husband.

Sophie is wearing what she at first thinks is a rosette or a brooch. It is pink. Then she realizes it is not a brooch at all but her own skin coming through her clothes. She describes it as a very graphic and disturbing image.

She is driving a lawn mower down the road and realizes that pieces of the mower are falling off and are strewn all over the road. She is worried about the safety of someone who is behind her on the road. She stops and tries to pick up the parts that have fallen off, but at that moment a woman approaches and tries to steal her handbag. Sophie manages to stop her.

I am fairly sure that the dream is connected with the previous day's session. I ask Sophie for her associations to the dream. She immediately refers to the second part and tells me that her skin broke out in ugly patches last night. She has a long-term skin disorder that has been particularly painful recently and for which she is being treated by a dermatologist.

I point out that she may have been angry with me for dropping off to sleep the day before but that she had protected me by blaming herself, and this may be why her skin problem has flared up. (At the same time, I am having my own unspoken associations to the first part of Sophie's dream: the senior teacher's [analyst's] ignoring her while paying attention to the new parents [cat]. I am also disturbed by the third part of her dream: the collapsing lawn mower.)

She agrees with my interpretation, which tells me that she was so depressed yesterday that she did not felt like creating a conflict with me. It then comes out that she had sensed that I was not properly paying attention and thought that I had probably fallen asleep. She had tested me by asking me in a very quiet voice whether I was okay. When I did not respond, she had said in a louder voice, which I did hear,

"Am I putting you to sleep?" I now realize that I had indeed dropped off as she surmised. I feel I have let Sophie down and have not lived up to my own high standards for myself.

Letting me off the hook, Sophie remarks: "But you came back to life. I just thought you were having a bad day."

I say, "It was as if you experienced me during those difficult moments as a dead mother who had abandoned you."

Sophie's association here was to the death of her mother some years ago. She had been the one who had to tell her grandmother the news. Worried about her grandmother's reactions, Sophie said to her, "Please, don't you die on me, too."

I tell Sophie that I believe that, even if only for a moment, she had thought she was going to lose me yesterday. Her protecting me meant that she did not have to be in touch with her reluctance to leave the session in case she might leave behind too many fragmented (lawn mower) aspects of herself in the room for my next patient.

Sophie nods and begins to cry, then tells me that, as a child, she had desperately wanted an animal to love and touch.

I realize at this moment that my preoccupation with the possible demise of my cat was not merely a neurotic countertransference but rather a coconstructed experience in which I unconsciously needed to be in touch in my body and my mind, through my own cat, with Sophie's devastation at the recent loss of her horse—the carrier of her neglected infant self, who needed to be emotionally touched. In the transference and corresponding countertransference, we could together find a connection between the little girl's longing for touch and her body's expression of disappointment and rage at its absence, which had led to long-term skin problems. Later I tell her that I was preoccupied with something that led me to fall asleep, but I do not tell her what it was.

I cannot go on being the soothing analyst for Sophie forever. Although I prefer not to incarnate for her a neglectful, anxious mother, and I consider my anxious countertransference as something of my own making in the session, this "bear" that disturbed her turned out to be a "bush in strange disguise." This happening eventually led to what Samuels would call my embodied countertransference and brought into consciousness a complex of Sophie's, the neglectful, untouchable mother, which had until then been well hidden.[34]

Countertransference and Imagination

My experience with Sophie began to arouse my curiosity about the way in which the process of countertransference actually works. What had happened within me and between Sophie and me that allowed me to transform with Sophie what I had first thought of as an intrusion of my own worry into the session (the disappearance of my cat) into a shared consciousness of a very early maternal failure in Sophie's childhood?

Some believe that the concept of projective identification provides an adequate explanation of these experiences. Rosemary Gordon, for example, suggests that the role of projective identification in the construction of countertransference reactions is based on the psychoid unconscious, in which distinctions between psyche and soma do not apply; this area of the unconscious is inaccessible to consciousness.[35] This is the place that Sophie and I were both compelled to visit that day. Ogden is more interested in the multidimensional nature of projective identification, which he characterizes as "a psychological process that is at once a type of defence, a mode of communication, a primitive form of object relationship and a pathway for psychological change."[36]

There is nothing I can disagree with in either of these conceptualizations, but, as Jungians, we have access to a more three-dimensional approach to countertransference. My experience with Sophie led me to wonder how the countertransference process relates to a capacity to imagine, and I believe that we can think of countertransference as a special form of active imagination that the analyst can use to make sense of patients' projections.

Resting on the psyche's archetypal capacity to form images, Jung's method of active imagination remained close to his heart throughout his working life.[37] Although Jung at first used it to scrutinize his own unconscious inner life, the method developed for him into one that had relevance for all analyses. My connection here turns out to be not entirely a new one. Davidson maintained that a successful analysis could be thought of as "a lived-through active imagination,"[38] and more recently, Schaverien too reframes countertransference-generated imagery as active imagination.[39] However, I do not believe that the process itself and the stages involved have been considered in any depth.

The *Oxford English Dictionary* defines imagination as follows: "The action of imagining or forming mental images or concepts of external objects not present to the senses." This implies that imagination involves *an active process* in which what one is imagining is differentiated from material reality. Warnock describes this process more elegantly: "Both artist and spectator have to detach themselves from the world in order to think of certain objects in the world in a new way, as signifying something else."[40] Both the artist and the spectator (the patient and the analyst) have to suspend their normal perceptions of the external world and their own intuitions, bodily sensations, and feelings so that something new can emerge, something that can be thought about in a new way. This brings to mind Samuel Johnson's humorous depiction of imagination: "Were it not for imagination, Sir, a man would be as happy in the arms of a chambermaid as of a Duchess."

Imagination was originally believed to reside in an actual place in the brain, as important as reason and memory, although in the post-Enlightenment period this was realized to be a rather naïve concept; as a result, brain and mind came to be studied separately.[41] The poets, particularly Coleridge and Wordsworth, then took on the mantle of imagination. Coleridge considered primary imagination to be the living agent of all perception and *a mental function* rather than a place in the mind. Secondary imagination was for him the echo of primary imagination but with a different mode of operation; he held that it dissolves, diffuses, and dissipates in order to re-create. In other words, secondary imagination makes sense of what one perceives.

I contend that imagination is *both a mental space and a mental function*. We use our imagination to create a mental space in order to make sense of internal and external experiences, and we then creatively scrutinize the images spontaneously formed in our mind in order to differentiate them from reality—a mental function. These two stages do not necessarily occur sequentially and may in fact overlap, but they sound remarkably like the process of countertransference. The following quotation from Mary Warnock is about imagination, but imagine for a moment that it is about countertransference:

> Meanings spring up around us as soon as we are conscious. The imagination is that which ascribes these meanings, which sees them *in* the objects before us, whether these are the ordinary three-dimensional furniture of the world, diagrams in a textbook, pictures, music, or images in the mind's eye or ear. At an everyday level, we must use imagination to apply concepts to things. This is the way we render the world familiar, and therefore manageable. . . . If, below the level of consciousness, our imagination is at work tidying up the chaos of sense experience, at a different level it may . . . untidy it again.[42]

Both imagination and countertransference require of the analyst not only a capacity to create a mental space *but also* to use a mental function. The analyst needs to create a space, a place in the mind, where something can happen. Britton refers to this as the "other room."[43] Countertransference takes place in the other room of the mind, a place that emerges from the right hemisphere to right hemisphere unconscious nonverbal relating between two people, where "meaning is not singularly discovered, but dyadically created."[44] This is similar to Bollas's idea of "countertransference readiness," the creation of an internal space that is experienced even if what will enter it is not yet known.[45] In this space we meet our patients' unconscious communications.

However, imagination is a mental function, as well as a mental space. Returning to Britton, "when we place our phantasies about events in this psychic 'other room' of our imagination, we know we are imagining something."[46] We need this mental function in order to know what we are imagining and then to be able to appraise and understand the meaning of what we are experiencing with a patient.

I am talking here about an active process that we use to make sense of unconscious communications that emerge between patient and analyst and that sound to me remarkably similar to Jung's method of active imagination:

> He must make the emotional state the basis or starting point of the procedure. He must make himself as conscious as possible of the mood he is in, sinking himself in it without reserve. . . . Fantasy must be allowed the freest possible play, yet not in such a manner that it leaves the orbit of its object, namely the affect. . . . The whole procedure is a kind of enrichment and clarification of the affect.[47]

Jung's method involves a readiness to experience emotions and images from the unconscious and then to come to terms with what they mean.[48] There are different forms of experience, including the somatic, the visual, and the auditory.

The idea that the analyst's countertransference involves a process similar to active imagination finds support among other authors. Heimann brings us more pragmatically into the consulting room by addressing the qualities and strength of the countertransference process in terms of three cognitive positions analysts may adopt:

1. a listening observer (attitude)
2. a partner in a special dialogue (involvement)
3. a supervisor of herself, sifting through patients' material and her own responses (appraisal)[49]

Heimann assumes that these are either-or options. I prefer, however, to see all three of her cognitive positions as essential and overlapping aspects of an active process of imagination, whereby analysts gradually become conscious of the strength and direction of the countertransference current with their patients.

There is first a "listening observer." This is our *attitude* toward the patient, which involves the creation of an internal space, a frame in which something can happen. There is then an experience of "a partner in a special dialogue," a particular kind of *involvement* between analysts and their patients, what Bollas calls "generative countertransference regression."[50] Of course, this is likely to vary from patient to patient. As analytical psychologists, we might reframe Bollas's "generative countertransference regression" in terms of the constant influence of unconscious archetypal forces. Heimann's third position, what she calls "the analyst as supervisor of herself sifting through patients' material and her own responses," suggests a process of continual *appraisal* by analysts of their own subjective experiences to find meaning that may later be verbalized to their patients. Appraisal may be linked to Fonagy's concept of reflective function,[51] a concept expanded by Knox to include analysts' awareness of their psychological separateness and individuality.[52]

These three central activities—our attitude toward our patients, the nature of our involvement, and our capacity for appraisal—together set the stage for analysts to develop the capability to make good use of their countertransference affects, what I consider to be a process of active imagination. They allow the analyst to "welcome news from within himself" from personal feelings, bodily responses, intuitions, images, and fantasies.[53] The difficult task, of course, is to discern which of these "news headlines" belong to the analyst and which come from patients' transference projections. These two related sources of information come to us in sessions with patients and permit the sifting that is essential to discovering which of our countertransference affects are reliable and which less so.

Heimann's three activities suggest three German verbs—*geschehen lassen, betrachten,* and *sich auseinandersetzen*—which Jung used to describe conscious activity in its confrontation with the unconscious. Elie Humbert has asserted that Jung's verbs evoke a process that can allow "the power of what is unknown within the unconscious to manifest itself without becoming possessed by it."[54]

Just a small step is required to extend Jung's usage of these three verbs to the process of countertransference:

a) *Geschehen lassen* means to let something happen with an attitude of tolerance. It is neither a state of abandon within which anything can occur nor a passive sort of "letting go," but it describes well the analyst's attitude toward and involvement with the patient.

b) *Betrachten* means "to become aware of the existence of something." This "something" begins to come into consciousness and can be reflected upon.

c) *Sich auseinandersetzen* means to confront oneself with something, to come to terms with it. Through a process of appraisal that involves the analyst's reflective function, meaning can be found.

What I have been describing as a process of active imagination *within* the analyst cannot be dissociated from what is happening *between* patient and analyst, which, of course, comes out of a shared space. Authors have found different metaphors to help us to imagine the character of this shared space. Winnicott refers to a third area of play that begins in infancy and develops into creative living throughout adult life.[55] He sees play as experience in the potential space between the individual and the environment, and how it develops depends on the degree of trust between mother and baby.

Ogden's shared space is described as an *analytic third* created by the interplay of subjectivity and intersubjectivity in the analytic setting: "The analytic experience occurs at the cusp of the past and the present and involves a 'past' that is being created anew [for both patient and analyst], by means of an experience generated between analyst and analysand [i.e., within the analytic third]."[56] Ogden views this analytic third as a framework for understanding ideas about the interdependence of subject and object, of transference and countertransference, where analysts sift through their bodily sensations and the ramblings of their mind as if they were clinical facts.

Schwartz-Salant's concept of the *interactive field* provides a more Jungian perspective on shared space; for him, it is a space that is larger than the patient and analyst and contains both of them: "The interactive field is in-between the field of the collective unconscious and the realm of subjectivity, while at the same time including them both."[57]

Finally, French philosopher Corbin puts forward the concept of *mundus imaginalis,* the world of the image. Corbin refers to "the organ which perceived the *mundus imaginalis*" as "imaginative consciousness," a state between waking and sleeping, where patient and analyst are linked by and can hopefully gain access to a central, imaginative function.[58]

The World through Blunted Sight

Patrick Trevor-Roper, a consultant eye surgeon, wrote an extraordinary book called *The World through Blunted Sight,* in which he examines the ways in which the unfocused images of painters, writers, and other artists with sight deficiencies seriously affected their perceptions and their work. The poet Milton, for example, was very short sighted and rarely mentions birds in his verses except for the nocturnal song of the nightingale. Tennyson's son Hallam wrote of his father's myopia: "He was so short-sighted that the moon without a glass seemed to him like a shield across the sky."[59] Tennyson's poetic interests, not surprisingly, turned to objects that he could view at close range.

As analysts, we, too, can encounter the world of our patients' experiences through blunted sight. Warnock reminds us that imagination is unreliable; it can make things untidy. Shakespeare, in the quotation at the beginning of this chapter, evoked the capacity of imagination for disguise: A beautiful bush sometimes turns out to be a frightening bear. With some irony Lord Macaulay highlights the limitations of imagination: "His imagination resembled the wings of an ostrich. It enabled him to run, though not to soar."[60] Colman contrasts an imaginative capacity that can lead to symbolization with what he calls the imaginary, a clinging to fantasy to avoid reality.[61] Thus, we can be misguided in our imaginings, and confusions between fantasy and reality can become disorienting. This is particularly so for trainees, who lack a sufficiently well-developed transcendent function that would enable them to use their countertransference imaginings fluently.

In my work with Sophie, the "other room" of my mind became blocked, filled with my dark imaginings about the fate of my cat. Falling asleep to relieve my anxiety blunted, albeit temporarily, my imaginative function. Was this just a neurotic countertransference reaction in which I turned briefly from a benign bush into a dangerous bear for Sophie, or was there an unconscious motivation for this lapse? Could it have served a purpose?

Jung maintains that the process of active imagination begins with a disturbing experience: "In the intensity of the emotional disturbance itself lies the value, the energy which he [the analyst] should have at his disposal in order to remedy the state of reduced adaptation."[62] It was only after Sophie alerted me to my drift into unconsciousness that I was able to make sense for myself and later with her of the deeper meaning of this enactment. I think she needed me to enact an aspect of her inner world—her internal mother—who had been anxious and taken rather poor care of her child. This enactment was a joint creation involving both my uncomfortable subjective responses and the projected aspects of Sophie's world in the transference. Although initially illusory, it ultimately turned into something syntonic,[63] but only after I found myself able to again find an imaginative mental space and function with which to discuss with her what was happening between us.

David Sedgwick contends that countertransference is always there even if we are not conscious of it, and he provides an evocative image for the concept of countertransference: "Psychotherapy is like a good-sized river, formed by two smaller rivers flowing together, and *countertransference is a continuous current in that river. It is not so much used as discovered and realized.*"[64]

In this chapter I have evoked the nature of this current and the process by which it can be discovered and realized, using a vignette of Sophie's analysis as my case example.

I began by tracing the history of the concept of countertransference and showing that it has evolved from something considered to be a contamination of the analyst's essential neutrality to (in the early twenty-first century) an invaluable tool in the analytic relationship to help the analyst make sense of patients' transference projections. I have discussed some of the ways that authors have found meaning in the nature and process of the concept of countertransference, drawing on what I consider to be seminal contributions from both analytical psychologists and psychoanalysts.

Jung intuitively grasped the significance of the analytic relationship and the effect that patient and analyst can have on one another, but his failure to flesh out for us in detail how he used it in his clinical work suggests that he may have used his countertransference affects in an educative way by telling patients what they evoked in him or turning to myths or stories to amplify an image in a dream or to fantasize with them.

I believe that analysts' imaginative use of their countertransference experiences can be a major therapeutic factor in analysis. If these affects remain unscrutinized, however, they can lead to dangerous enactments and impasse. We use our feelings, our bodily responses, our thoughts, our images, and our dreams to understand our patients. This often involves states of unconscious identification where we become mixed up with our patients. The countertransference, like transference, has to be lived before it can be understood (Wordsworth talks of "the mysterious power of imagination"). Because our sight can, on occasion, become seriously blunted, the countertransference is to be trusted but treated with great caution.

In trying to grasp the nature of the countertransference process and how we and our trainees can use it effectively and with discrimination, I have suggested that the process is activated within a shared space variously described as an interactive field or an analytic third. It is most usefully viewed as a form of active imagination that requires both a mental space and a mental function—two different psychological states. Mental space involves a capacity to tune in sensitively to our patients. The mental function of imagination gives form to our imaginings and fantasies and helps us to retain an observing function that can reflect on the here-and-now impact of the events in the consulting room, as well as the broader picture.

With Sophie, I needed to unpack my own countertransference affects and to sift through possible unresolved shadow complexes of my own before I could find a way to respond authentically. This dual activity of entering into something while at the same time maintaining an observing function is difficult (some would say impossible). We are then, I believe, in the territory of Jung's transcendent function, a process where opposites can dialogue and engage in mutual influence, transcending old positions to find a new position attached to the ego. The process of imagination, involving as it does both a mental space and a mental function, is essential in this activity.

Shakespeare's words opened this chapter, so I let him have the last word, too. I have used my "poet's pen" to give to the concept of countertransference a "local habitation and a name"—an active process of imagination. It comes not from "airy nothing" but from the perspective of a Jungian analyst practicing in London in a culture where analytical psychology and psychoanalysis dovetail in this area. I hope I have left you with something that has triggered your imagination, but if not, I recommend to you Puck's words in the epilogue of *A Midsummer Night's Dream*:

> If we shadows have offended,
> Think but this and all is mended:
> That you have but slumber'd here,
> While these visions did appear.

CHAPTER 4

The Transference Matrix

Emotions are contagious because they are deeply rooted in the sympathetic system . . . any process of an emotional kind immediately arouses a similar process in others. . . . Even if the doctor is entirely detached from the emotional contents of the patient, the very fact that the patient has emotions has an effect on him. And it is a great mistake if the doctor thinks he can lift himself out of it. He cannot do more than become conscious of the fact that he is affected.

— C. G. Jung, "The Tavistock Lectures"

This remarkable quotation from Jung in lecture five of the Tavistock lectures brings home with great clarity Jung's sharp, intuitive understanding of the conscious and unconscious effects two people have on one another. He knew about transference in his bones, the archetypal nature of unconscious processes alive between patient and analyst, the emotional impact of analysis, and its potential for making meaning.

As part of his legacy, Jung left us with a visual amplification of the transference, known as the *marriage quaternity* in alchemy and the *gate model* in common parlance.[1] It shows the potentially complex conscious and unconscious relationship within patient and analyst and also between them (see figure 1).

Later authors such as Lambert, Kirsch, and Perry have developed Jung's diagram to take into account more explicitly the inevitable effects on the analyst of the patient's transferences,[2] as well as the analyst's transference onto the patient, what Jung called the "counter-crossing transference relationships."[3] (See figures 2 and 3 respectively)

The point about Jung's "counter-crossing transference relationships" is that they are both intrapsychic *and* interpersonal. He takes account not only of the patient's and the analyst's relationships with their own unconscious contents but also of the effects they have on one another. We are each open to experiences within ourselves and between us and others. However, Jung was particularly interested in a model of the mind that is generally concerned with higher states of mental functioning, including thinking, creativity, and the symbolic attitude, especially for patients in the later stages of their lives. Despite his acknowledgment of both the intrapsychic and the interpersonal, his methods seem to have developed in a lopsided way. They exhibit greater clarity and systematic study of his ways of thinking about archetypal imagery and intrapsychic communications from the unconscious in dreams and fantasies. However, his methods also reflect a rather vaguer approach to the clinical manifestations of embodied transference (e.g., why the analyst feels sleepy with one particular patient; forgets a session; suddenly feels hungry). These became subsumed under the rubric of the centrality of the analyst's personality rather than happenings between patient and analyst with a specific purpose and meaning that merit exploration within the transference. Jung was inclined to bypass the developmental phases of early life and their effects in adulthood, and, not surprisingly, this has been taken up by later authors. James Astor claims that filling in this gap is one of Fordham's great achievements:

> [It] give[s] Jungians their childhood and a way of thinking about it and analysing it—not as one aspect of the archetypal relationship but as a basis for the analysis of the transference within archetypal forms. It is not that he has put childhood in place of the impersonal archetypal features of analysis, so much as he has shown how the psyche oscillates between states of mind—sometimes mature, sometimes immature—which continue with greater or lesser strength throughout the life of the individual.[4]

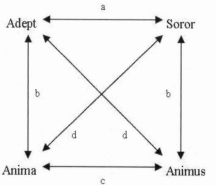

Fig. 1

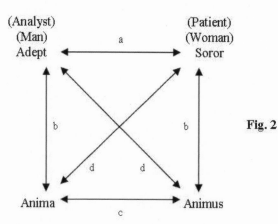

Fig. 2

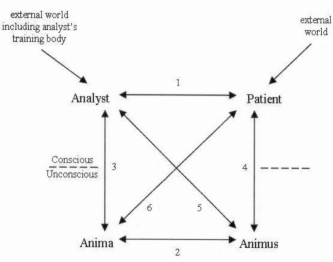

Fig. 3
The analytic or
"marriage" quaternio

At the age of seventy-one, Jung published *The Psychology of the Transference.*[5] He had found an alchemical text, the *Rosarium Philosophorum,* that triggered his imagination in a way that excited him. It became his model for thinking about the process of individuation, including a visual amplification of transference and the unfolding of an unconscious relationship between the patient and the analyst. Jung believed that transference was archetypal and that patterns could be observed going beyond the personal. In her thoughtful elaboration of this complex work of Jung's, Jean Kirsch describes how objective data from the world of alchemy became for Jung the scaffolding for the symbolism of the transference. In several stages she explores the production of the lapis, or the philosopher's stone, which for Jung became a key symbol of what analysis could achieve—individuation and the emergence of the self.[6]

The ten woodcuts that compose the *Rosarium* pictures date from 1550 and tell a love story—an incestuous one—between king and queen, using a symbolic bath, the *vas mirabile,* an alchemical vessel to contain the process and to depict the water of the unconscious, in which changes have the potential to take place. The woodcuts tell the story of the transformation of base metals into gold—the alchemists' aim. Although the complex imagery of the woodcuts is intellectually fascinating and absorbing, it is easy to get lost in it since it diverts the reader from the nuances of the human and more personal aspects of relationships. The pictures fall into five main categories that are parallel to the evolution of the alchemical process:

1. *divisio/solutio/separatio,* representing beginnings and the separation of the elements (pictures 1–3)

2. *coniunctio,* a union of opposites involving immersion and a loss of boundaries (pictures 4–5)

3. *nigredo,* a blackening suggestive of chaos and mistrust (pictures 6–7)

4. *mundificatio,* a process of purification, which involves a gradual coming down to earth (pictures 8–9)

5. *albedo,* a whitening with new discoveries and transformation, the philosopher's stone (picture 10)

PICTURE 1: THE MERCURIAL FOUNTAIN

This woodcut depicts the beginning of a journey, which is as yet unknown. The figures are not yet represented in the woodcut, and something distant, almost virginal, is conveyed. It is a symbolic representation of the theory and practice of analysis and, metaphorically, the beginning of an analysis.

PICTURE 2: THE KING AND THE QUEEN

The second woodcut introduces the two protagonists in the analytic relationship with the potential to fall in love with one another. The incestuous pull between them is present, as well as the dangers of either too much body or too much spirit. The contact between the left hands of the figures was, for Jung, suggestive of the possibility of something sinister in the relationship.

PICTURE 3: THE NAKED TRUTH

In the third woodcut, the king and the queen (patient and analyst) are undressed, seen without their respective personas. The dove watches over them while also affecting their relationship, suggestive of the need for trust and faith in the process of analysis as the potential for periods of unconscious identity becomes stronger. This woodcut refers to the sufficiently good therapeutic alliance necessary to contain unconscious forces as they emerge in analysis. It likely represents unconscious intersubjectivity.

PICTURE 4: IMMERSION IN THE BATH

The erotic aspect of this woodcut is obvious with all of the attendant danger of patient and/or analyst potentially losing the "as if" quality of the analysis. Questions arise about the viability of the vas, or container, to contain feelings of exposure, regression, dependency, potential fusion, and states of projective identification. Both the dove and the water are present, suggesting different kinds of connection. The atmosphere is one of excited anticipation, and the unconscious connection is deeper: archetypal, as well as personal.

PICTURE 5: THE CONIUNCTIO

To the uneducated eye, this woodcut is surely evocative of the sexual relationship between the king and the queen (analyst and patient). However, Jung is keen to point out the following:

> They were drawn for medieval eyes and . . . consequently they have a symbolical rather than a pornographic meaning. Medieval hermeneutics and meditation could contemplate even the most delicate passages in the Song of Songs without taking offence and view them through a veil of spirituality.[7]

The incestuous couple do indeed have wings. The picture suggests that the unconscious union of patient and analyst has taken place. The honeymoon is over, and they are now in a state of participation mystique, what we might today call *unconscious identity*. They are caught up in something bigger than both of them, and their union is deep and transpersonal.

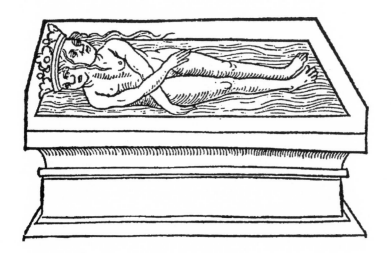

PICTURE 6: DEATH

This woodcut portrays the darkest time in an analysis. It suggests a psychological descent, called *nigredo* by the alchemists. We might guess that this stage of the analysis is characterized by loss of energy and perhaps by (mutual) disillusion with the process. Perry talks of empathic failure, which in his view can ultimately be therapeutic, providing analysts have the patience and skill to remain attentive to their self-analysis during this time.[8]

PICTURE 7: THE ASCENT OF THE SOUL

King and queen remain in the same dark place, yet an infant is rising from their tomblike container. Jung asserted that this can be one of the most difficult stages in an analysis: "This picture corresponds psychologically to a dark state of disorientation.... This collapse and disorientation of consciousness may last a long time ... demanding the greatest patience, courage and faith on the part of both doctor and patient."[9] The infant that is rising could connote persistent states of (possibly malign?) regression while at the same time connoting hope for the future.

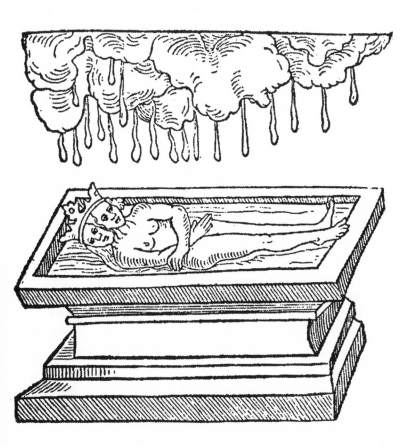

PICTURE 8: COMING BACK TO EARTH

Woodcut 8 conveys some movement and a time of change. The falling dew on the couple is helping to wash away the darkness, suggesting possible new insights about unconscious aspects of patient, analyst, or their relationship. Because the oppressive blackness is no longer present, feeling and thinking can return, heralding internal change. The cleansing water from the heavens signals the potential for new life.

PICTURE 9: RETURN OF THE SOUL

Here, the infant is depicted returning with verve and energy toward the couple. It is a stage full of promise, where opposites seem about to come together, producing further insights and withdrawal of projections for the patient and mutual satisfaction for both patient and analyst in the analytic work. It is a time when distinctions between what is personal and what is archetypal in the transference relationship can be explored and mutually appreciated. Of the two birds in the picture, one seems to be emerging from the ground; the other is there already. Jung believed them to be a pair of opposites, suggesting perhaps some ambivalence about change.

PICTURE 10: THE NEW BIRTH

Jung liked this final woodcut because, for him, it evoked the individual's capacity to produce symbols of the self: "The self is the total, timeless man and as such corresponds to the original, spherical, bisexual being who stands for the mutual integration of conscious and unconscious."[10] Jung saw this last woodcut as paradoxical; a two-headed hermaphrodite seems to be looking in two different directions (consciousness and unconsciousness?), suggesting integration, development, and a well-travelled journey. At the same time, however, a darker presence is embodied by a snake, as well as a raven, which Jung saw as "a synonym for the devil."[11] The woodcut suggests achievements and the potential for further experiences, both positive and negative, as well as a destination not yet reached, implying a continuing journey. The images of the snake and the raven could imply some (but by no means total) integration of the shadow.

It is clear that the imagery of the king and the queen in the alchemical bath has captured Jung's imagination as an evocation of the analytic process, and his studies of the alchemists' work constitute a major section of *The Psychology of the Transference*. In Jung's own words:

> To give any description of the transference phenomenon is a very difficult and delicate task, and I did not know how to set about it except by drawing upon the symbolism of the alchemical opus. The *theoria* of alchemy, as I think I have shown, is for the most part, a projection of unconscious contents, of those archetypal forms which are characteristic of all pure fantasy-products, such as are to be met with in myths and fairy-tales, or in the dreams, visions and the delusional systems of individual men and women. ... it did not seem to me too rash to use an historical document, whose substance derives from centuries of mental effort, as the basis and guiding thread of my argument.[12]

Jung conveys with some humility, then, that his use of alchemy as a metaphor for the unfolding transference is an experiment: "The problems connected with the transference are so complicated and so various that I lack the categories necessary for a systematic account."[13] He acknowledged, too, in his epilogue to the *Rosarium*, not only that the alchemists were rather vague about the stages described but also that it would be possible to set up various other working models of the transference.

I have taken Jung at his word, and my intention in this chapter is to suggest an alternative model for the emerging transference-and-countertransference relationship between patient and analyst that will honor Jung's central and valuable contributions while taking account of new developments and alternative perspectives. Jung's account of the transference based on illustrations from the *Rosarium Philosophorum* was published in 1946, and we now know more about transference and countertransference phenomena both theoretically and clinically. Jung's startling statement in the quotation at the beginning of this chapter (i.e., that "emotions are contagious") finds convincing evidence in contemporary research findings from the fields of both neuroscience and attachment theory (see chapter 2). Fordham has given us a theory of development that involves a self with a dynamic, prospective function that is active in infancy with energy that begins in utero and reaches out for experiences of relationship through a process of what he calls deintegration and reintegration.[14]

Fordham has also provided us with detailed case studies of emotional experiences in analysis and an appreciation of the nuances of meaning to be found in the bodily sensations, thoughts, and other affects that emerge in the transference and countertransference for both patient and analyst. Fordham's interest in infancy honors Jung's belief in the continuity of the self throughout life and its ability to survive all kinds of pleasurable and painful experiences, thereby giving us a Jungian model of development that is missing from Jung's own writing. I suggest that we need a new model of transference and countertransference that does not betray Jung's interest in the symbolic and the archetypal roots of transference but at the same time pays greater attention to personal psychopathology and its effects on interpersonal dynamics.

One difficulty with the *Rosarium* as a model of the transference has to do with whether it is really about the specifics of transference or rather a more general metaphor for individuation as a whole and the emergence of the self. In my experience, the described stages are overdetermined and prone to idealization. Although I believe we can all recognize in broad terms the process of development illustrated in the *Rosarium* pictures, patients can become "stuck" at an early stage for many years or move back and forth between different stages. The linear qualities of the process can be misleading.

A second and more troublesome question concerns the clinical usefulness of Jung's model and whether it serves clinicians effectively today. It paints with broad strokes, but it is insufficient to help us find meaning in the varied presentations, states, of mind, and moods of our patients. It raises once more the question of the extent to which

Jung paid only lip service to the transference and countertransference in his clinical work. We cannot know for sure how much he engaged interpersonally with patients who could not symbolize, regressed during their analysis, or needed analysis as a physical and an emotional space within which to engage with primitive processes likely to place intense demands on the analyst. I suspect that, for Jung, transformations came for the most part in other ways, including the analysis and amplification of dreams, as well as the use of active imagination.

The Capacity for Symbolization

In preparation for and as an introduction to my own model of the transference, I invite the reader first to consider the following quotations from two authors writing almost forty years apart. The first is by Fred Plaut (1966), and the second by Gustav Bovensiepen (2002).

Plaut paraphrases Jung: "A reliance on images alone leads into a kind of desert unless associated with analysis of personal relationships." Later in the same article, he states that "the capacity to form images and to use these constructively by re-combination into new patterns is dependent on the individual's capacity to trust. . . . *Failure in this area impoverishes life and requires careful transference analysis in order to further the ego's function to trust both in relationships and in one's imagination.*"[15]

Bovensiepen puts it a little differently: "If the symbolic attitude is primarily understood as a relational process instead of an intellectual amplification of symbolic contents, this understanding would expand our treatment options for patients who are, above all, plagued by difficulties with symbolization." He also emphasizes that "Jung's prospective function of the living symbol, which he stressed repeatedly, corresponds to the need for a living object."[16]

From these two eminent analytical psychologists we learn that the analytic relationship, the person of the analyst, and transference analysis together promote a symbolic capacity. We hope that our own personality is sufficiently developed to help our patients acquire an imaginative capacity for play that will lead them to think about what they lack or what they have lost. Nonetheless, using our personality alone is not enough. To learn how to do this work, we need a variety of competencies and a method that is flexible and sensitive enough for all of our patients. We must learn how to combine an approach that takes account of our patients' stage of development, uses transference appropriately, and also gives sustained attention to content such as images and symbols. For some patients, especially those with early disturbance, difficulties *have* to be worked out first in the transference relationship: "The transcendent function does not work spontaneously but requires a matrix which is based on the child's earliest experience of a relationship and which can later be re-enacted in the treatment."[17]

Plaut's and Bovensiepen's views are essential to my argument. I suggest first that we consider the symbolic attitude as a relational process in which living symbols herald new meanings that emerge in living relationships and play an important role in the transference. Second, although Jung held that the symbol-making capacity of the psyche is a natural, archetypal process, many of our patients cannot use their imaginative abilities. They become blocked, and it is only within an authentic relationship where trust can evolve and real connections happen in the transference that the self begins to emerge and, with it, the potential to trust in new relationships and in an internal capacity to make meaning.

The Transference Matrix

It may be that throughout this book I have exaggerated the significance of the different attitudes toward transference observable in the Jungian world. Indeed, there may now be a greater overlap of approach to both theory and clinical practice than there was some years ago. I hope so, and in a spirit of inquiry that tries to bring together different approaches to the psyche, I suggest a contemporary metaphor for transference that retains both the importance of the symbolic and the profound effect that patient and analyst have can on one another. It acknowledges, too, recent writing in the fields of infant research, neuroscience, and emergence theory, as well as more detailed clinical studies of different kinds of transference.

I suggest that we adopt the term *transference matrix* as a contemporary Jungian metaphor that refers to a coconstructed place with structure, form, and energy. The term offers us a framework for thinking about transference, countertransference, and the making of meaning in analysis. The transference matrix is a structure that contains the psyche's capacity for both relating and creating, including the role of the other to facilitate or, in some cases, to obstruct development. This metaphor has the potential to bring together in a more integrated way approaches that until now have favored either a developmental or a symbolic emphasis.

The term *matrix* comes from the Latin word for "womb," a place of origin where babies are carried, protected, and nourished until ready to emerge into the world. The *Oxford English Dictionary* defines the word *matrix* as "a place or point of origin and growth; a mould in which something is cast or shaped; a mass of fine-grained rock in which gems, crystals, or fossils are embedded." With these definitions in mind, one may see the transference matrix as an environment that can enable personal transferences to emerge, including the infantile, as well as the precious, archetypal pearls that come from the self.

Winnicott referred to ego-relatedness as the "matrix of transference" and saw the mother as the infant's psychological matrix.[18] My use of the term *transference matrix* begins as a twosome, a place of potential relationship from the beginning, in which the analyst maintains a free-floating awareness of the different levels of patients' experience, including the developmental and the archetypal, with space for the not-yet-known. The matrix is a structure that contains the analytic pair like a womb or a mould and provides the potential bedrock for a process to evolve. It also has its own energy and power, which are greater than the combination of the two people within it.

Bringing together research from the fields of neurobiology and attachment theory, Siegel writes about the neurobiological processes that facilitate the emergence of mind from brain activity that takes place when interacting with other brains and minds. His ideas help to provide a biological foundation for what I am calling the transference matrix. Siegel states that "it is within the vital human connections of interpersonal relationships that many of the neural connections which create the mind are shaped: human relationships shape the brain structure from which the mind emerges."[19]

He describes the undifferentiated brain as a system (biological matrix) made up of layers that evolve from the creation of neural pathways as synapses form. These synapses "allow for the creation of these component parts to become differentiated and to carry out such features as attention, perception, memory and emotional regulation. . . . It is for this reason that the early years of life, the time when the basic circuits of the brain are becoming established that mediate such processes as emotional and behavioral regulation, interpersonal relatedness, language and memory, are the most crucial for the individual to receive the kinds of experience that enable proper development to occur."[20]

I find myself wanting to link Jung's "gate" model of "counter-crossing transference relationships" with Siegel's idea that the brain is actually socially dependent. Not only do two people—mother and baby or patient and analyst—have the capacity to influence one another's psyches and emotions, but "interpersonal experience may continue to influence neurobiological processes throughout the lifespan" as well.[21] It could be said, then, that affect has the power to regulate experience, but affect is also regulated *by* it in turn—a truly interactive matrix of connections. Jung's view that psychic energy flows through different channels—biological, psychological, spiritual, and moral—finds support from Siegel's notion of mind as coming from the specific patterns in the flow of energy and information within a single individual and between individuals: "In this way the mind is created both by neurological processes within the individual and interpersonal interactions between them."[22] He is talking about self-regulating circuits that form in infancy that are dependent on experience. There is not just an interpersonal psychology but also an interpersonal neurology.

What of the process within the transference matrix? Cambray, in a chapter called "Emergence and the Self," looks at holism in science through the concept of emergence. Tracing philosophical and scientific developments over the past four centuries, Cambray thinks of Jung's model of the psyche as a form of field theory: "an interactive field model emerging from a background archetypal field." He investigates a strand of holistic thinking known as *dynamic systems theory* and highlights self-organizing systems that he characterizes as emergent. Emergent phenomena, he asserts, are likely to make themselves felt at the edge of order and chaos. As a way of helping the reader to understand these adaptive systems, Cambray uses the analogy of airports in major cities as interconnected hubs and the smaller town and city airports that link up with the larger hubs as nodes. An analysis of the patient's complexes from childhood—major hubs—have the capacity to move them on to more subtle nodal patterns that connect at the unexplored edges of experience in analysis.[23]

Cambray's description of these moments of emergence of the self, where the symmetry in the system is broken, is intrinsic to change. While characteristic of the self in development, they presumably happen in the transference, the very individual and complex system of interactions of selves when patient and analyst meet in the consulting room. His emphasis[24] on the crucial affect of surprise in emergence is reminiscent of Stern's "moments of meeting."[25] Cambray's ideas permit us to think about the process and phases that arise within the transference matrix. Inevitably there will be times of unconscious identity, what Jung called *participation mystique*, where both parties are caught up in something unconscious, not yet understood but capable of leading to emergent moments, changes in the shape of the system, which often happen without warning or reason and bring new experiences and insights. Solomon, too, is interested in emergence theory:

The theory of emergent properties, also known as emergence theory . . . has recently developed as a tool in understanding how, across all matter, a deep structural dynamic at the edge of chaos is at work in which order, pattern and, psychologically speaking, systems of meaning threaten to break down into chaos. Under the right conditions, a structural transformation into a more complex pattern or meaning may occur.[26]

My concept of the transference matrix has some similarity with Martin-Vallas's concept of the transference chimera, which proposes that, in the analysis, energy is released autonomously, creating a shared space for analytic experience.[27] Martin-Vallas contends that this space is archetypal and activated in different ways in different analyses. The chimera and the transference are multifaceted like the chimera in Greek mythology—a fire-breathing monster that has a lion's head, a goat's body, and a snake's tail.

To end this chapter I recommend to the reader an absorbing account of two analyses from different perspectives by both analyst and patient. With some initiative, the *Journal of Analytical Psychology* in 2007 and 2008 published three articles with commentaries. They are unusual for two reasons. First of all, Astor, in an article titled "Fordham, Feeling, and Countertransference: Reflections on Defences of the Self," writes about the analysis of one of Fordham's patients, called simply "K."[28] During analysis, an impasse was reached, and the sessions ended. Some time later, Astor took "K" into analysis himself. Second, in two very moving articles "K" reflects thoughtfully about his experience in analysis with first Fordham and then Astor.[29] These articles vividly portray my concept of the transference matrix. In analysis, where, in Jung's words at the beginning of the chapter, "emotions are contagious," events can unfold in very different ways. Astor maintains that K's analysis with Fordham could have reached an impasse not because of any incompetence or lack of insight on Fordham's part but because Fordham had an unresolved difficulty with his own father, which led to a blind spot in his analysis of "K," who also had an extremely problematic relationship with his own father. Periods of unconscious identity, in which both parties became caught up in a place of unknowing did not lead to "moments of meeting" or emergence, where meaning could be found and connection experienced. After years of analysis, "K" remained in extreme pain. Astor argues that this tells us something about the areas in which we often fail at "finding the right way to say what we mean."[30] Later, when in analysis with Astor, "K" felt recognized, accepted, and understood, he said, "I find such connectedness-in-feeling helpful. One isn't alone. That's a burden less. That someone else can be affected by what one says lends substance and reality to one's feelings. It confers, however briefly, a sense of self and of identity. It makes one feel recognised.

It opens the possibility of being understood. It is host to reciprocation."[31]

Astor, with the benefit of a long collegial and personal relationship with Fordham, was sufficiently flexible to try something different. He and Fordham also had different personalities. Later in the same article, "K" refers to "discrete moments of becoming" in his analysis with Astor, what I take to be experiences of emergence within the transference and countertransference relationship between patient and analyst.

Our patients' various needs require us to find an appropriate language to say what we mean, but this is not always possible since the matrix of transference/countertransference relatedness inevitably involves periods of unconsciousness and sometimes occasions in which the analyst's limits and limitations make themselves felt. In this case, it appears that "K" required his analyst to recognize, accept, and understand his feelings rather than work in detail with the transference. This leads naturally to questions of differences in analytic method and to the final chapter in the book.

CHAPTER 5

Transference for Life

KEEPING THE PATIENT IN MIND

Destiny itself is like a wonderful wide tapestry in
which every thread is guided by an unspeakably ten-
der hand, placed beside another thread, and held and
carried by a hundred others.

— Rilke, *Letters to a Young Poet*

This quote from Rainer Maria Rilke is from one of his ten letters to
the young poet Franz Kappus in April 1903. These letters, which are
some of the most famous ever written, constitute a profound exchange
between two people who touched one another emotionally for a
period of five years, during which time they wrote about the potential
to live a creative life. The threads are always there, says Rilke, but they
need an "unspeakably tender hand" to guide them. I now come to
the last of my five chapters. First I gather up some of the threads of
my thoughts and arguments developed in the first four chapters. In
doing so I hope to make a reasonably appealing psychological tapestry, a contemporary and more coherent underpinning for a Jungian
approach to transference that will be relevant to practicing analytical
psychologists in the twenty-first century.

Revisiting the Themes of the Book

In chapter 1, from the starting point of Jung's definition of transference
as the noun *Übertragung*, which refers to the unconscious carrying of
something from one place to another, I differentiate Jung's teleological
emphasis on transference as the projection of what is not yet known

from the more Freudian emphasis on transference as the return of the repressed. Jung's attitude toward the psyche and the unconscious as normally dissociated—a vertical division—and his interest in the unrepressed, collective unconscious with its natural symbol-making capacity, is altogether different from Freud's horizontal division, in which he viewed repression as an unconscious, defensive maneuver and a more pathological form of functioning.

Jung's inconsistent views about transference and his tendency to swing between specific definitions, as well as his more general use of the term to describe the analytic relationship in its entirety, are confusing. The fascinating early letters exchanged between Jung and Freud in 1909 suggest that Jung's vulnerability to the powerful erotic transference he experienced with Sabina Spielrein, his first analytic patient, may have made him wary of too close a personal involvement with his patients. Whereas Freud and post-Freudians were drawn increasingly toward an interest in the nuances of transference dynamics in the analytic relationship, Jung, after the collapse of his relationship with Freud, was happier working with his beloved dreams and the archetypal images and symbols that emerged from the unconscious.

Facing the discomfort of Jung's ambivalence, analytical psychologists took a variety of transference directions in their working methods, which were, of course, influenced by the trends and personalities prevalent in local cultures. Some (and I include myself) turned to a developmental approach as a result of their interest in the formation of complexes even in the earliest stages of life and also specifically in Fordham's ideas about the development of the self in infancy. Psychoanalytic perspectives were essential to understanding the subtleties of the analytic relationship and the way they might vary among patients. Others chose to follow Jung's central ideas more closely since they were convinced that Jung offered future analysts a good enough method with which to work with patients. This has unfortunately led to two transference camps—the developmental and the classical—a division that endures today. For those interested in the developmental approach, relating and its processes have taken precedence, whereas for those more interested in a classical approach, gaining access to the contents and creative energy of the collective unconscious have taken on greater significance. These rather different approaches to the unconscious have led to radical divisions in terms of methods of practice involving transference.

From my own perspective, patients need the kind of relationship with their analysts that provides constant attention to process, including the transference, so that the archetypal energy necessary for development can be harnessed *in* a relationship. It is within the framework of an authentic relationship with the analyst's "unspeakably tender hand" that new images are likely to surface when the unconscious eventually facilitates an internal capacity to make meaning.

In chapter 2 I discuss some of the controversies about transference that have led to diverse approaches to working methods. In particular, I focus on a view of transference as the total situation,[1] a popular approach in the United Kingdom. It was developed by Kleinian analysts who believed that the only way to gain access to primitive states of mind and the unconscious was to make use of the here-and-now of the transference relationship. Because everything has a meaning in the transference, it gives clues to the patient's earliest, unconscious fantasies. While acknowledging a central role for transference, I questioned whether everything that emerges from the psyche within the analytic relationship comes only from these earliest states of mind. I also reflected with some suspicion about the effects on our patients of what might seem to be relentless transference interpretations from an analyst listening with a prejudiced ear to patients' communications.

Second, I unpacked Jung's possible intention when he advocated a central role for the analyst's personality in the analytic relationship, a question that seems to become more complicated the deeper we delve. Of course, the analyst's personality influences the progress of an analysis, but we need to use our personality differently with different patients. Some need a more active or challenging analyst, whereas others benefit from a quieter, more recessive state of being. Analysts must have the necessary training and experience to recognize their patients' different needs and how these may change over time. It is easy to confuse the benefits of authenticity, in which analysts make themselves fully available to their patients—both psychologically and emotionally—with the dangers of too "real" a relationship, which compromises the analytic and ethical attitude and makes it difficult to maintain a nonjudgmental, safe psychic container in which patients may discover more about themselves.

Transference is a natural, archetypal, multidirectional process that is both complex and extremely subtle. It brings about various and sometimes contrasting transferences, including the erotic, the psychotic, the negative, the idealizing, and the addictive, and sometimes it seems to be absent altogether. What is transferred is always unconscious: a complex stirred in the present with roots in the patient's past; a mood of the moment, not yet conscious to the patient; an internal object projected into the analyst; an infantile anxiety or fantasy; and then suddenly something new and archetypal, activated for the first time within the analytic relationship, like Stern's "moments of meeting."[2] Each of these transference projections has the potential to activate the analyst's countertransference affects in different ways and, if carefully processed and returned to the patient in a manageable form, can lead to new insights.

We are helped in our efforts to create a framework for thinking about transference by making a central distinction between working *in* the transference and working *with* it. Whether we like it or not, we are always working *in* the transference. The evidence from neuroscience, attachment theory, and infant research shows clearly that subjectivity is an emergent and interactive process. We affect each other from cradle to grave, and the quality of our earliest relationships is likely to influence the biochemistry and the structure of the brain by creating neural pathways connected to emotions that establish essential patterns for adult relationships. Those of our patients who have experienced a mother capable of mediating and regulating her baby's emotions are more likely to develop internal capacities to soothe and manage themselves when in distress. Other patients who lack the experience of a mother who tuned in to their emotions remain easily upset and volatile. They develop either the "hot" responses typical of borderline or psychotic states of mind or the "colder," distant reactions of those who have shut themselves off from relationships, thereby leaving themselves isolated but protected from frightening intrusions. Let me again quote Schore's wise words:

"Meaning is not singularly discovered but dyadically created."[3] Working *with* the transference—deciding when and how to interpret our patients' transference projections—has led to a diversity of methods of practice throughout the Jungian world.

In chapter 3 I build a meaningful connection between the concept of countertransference and the texture of the imaginative process. There I relate Jung's concept of active imagination to the process that allows analysts to recognize and reflect upon their bodily responses, fantasies, thoughts, and feelings experienced as a result of interactions with their patients. Using the countertransference involves the analyst in a dual process: first, a letting go, a receptive state of being that creates an inner space much like meditation or reverie in order to remain open to patient's projections. Then follows a more active state of imaginatively engaging with what has been received, as well as a more ego-oriented process of appraisal of its purpose and meaning. With reference to the ideas of British philosopher Mary Warnock, I also show that the capacity to imagine involves (in much the same way as analysts' capacity to make good use of their countertransference affects) both a mental state and a mental function. It requires considerable skill and experience to simultaneously maintain a receptive frame of mind (with the possibility of being taken over by feelings evoked by patients), retain an analytic attitude, and continue to function as an observer.

Chapter 4 describes Jung's major text on transference, in which he draws in detail on the *Rosarium Philosophorum,* a visual amplification of the transference, individuation, and the unconscious processes at work between patient and analyst, using the ancient science of alchemy as his metaphor. The work, drawing as it does on a series of woodcuts with complicated imagery is not to everyone's taste and seems from one perspective to be more about the stages of individuation than about transference and countertransference per se. It is best known for Jung's diagram of the "counter-crossing transference relationship" called the marriage quaternio in alchemy.[4] The highlight of Jung's work in this area is his emphasis on both the conscious and the unconscious relationship between patient and analyst, as well as the need (as evoked in the relationship between king and queen in the woodcuts) for both to "undress" if the process is to come to life and evolve.

Building on Jung's ideas but also cautious about his metaphor as too broad and intellectual in its references, I offer my own metaphor of *the transference matrix*, a coconstructed place and framework for thinking about transference and countertransference that allows for learning through experience within a relationship. The term *matrix*, suggesting as it does, a womb or place of origin, as well as a mould containing gems, crystals, or fossils, evokes the personal *and* the archetypal aspects of the transference. The matrix—because it has its own life and energy—is autonomous. It has a structure that hopefully contains the relationship and also a form unique to each analysis and the particular personalities of patient and analyst. This open system has a biological base for creating space not only for the infantile transference, including periods of regression and unconscious identity, but also for prescient imagery and the emergence of a symbolic capacity.

Relating and Creating

These are the main threads of argument in this book. Now comes the task of trying to weave them together. I have presented you with threads of different hues and textures: relating or creating; process or content; working *with* or working *in*, to name but a few. Weaving requires attention to questions of method, in particular several gaps in Jung's methods of studying the process of individuation.

I am sure you have gathered by now that working with the transference and the countertransference can be life enhancing, but if misused (as my chapter title "Transference for Life" implies), it can also become a life sentence that imprisons patients in a kind of strait jacket that has more to do with their analysts' dogmatic and misplaced views. There are the consequent dangers that patients will learn their analysts' language and that subsequent interactions will become artificial rather than authentic. David Bell remarked that transference can easily become a fetishized object for trainees, who believe that they will be in trouble if they fail to report regular transference interpretations in supervision: "It becomes degraded into a kind of fetish which I call 'giving the transference interpretation.' This being given not as a sign of understanding but a ritualised procedure serving to deal with anxiety, placate the supervisor, an action which replaces understanding."[5] This is a far cry from the hope that analysts in training will develop an "unspeakably tender hand" by using their transcendent function in a flexible and sensitive way with each of their patients. Bell's comment is not just about trainees, as it is surely their teachers who set the transference tone.

Rilke's words at the beginning of this chapter express an essentially Jungian theme—destiny in Rilke's terms is like the unfolding of the psyche with hope and purpose, where everything, even the smallest of happenings, carries significance. The analyst brings two threads together, knowing that what is created is ultimately dependent on the hundred other threads of potential that are waiting to be interwoven. Analysts help their patients weave connections between the personal and the collective. This process underpins what I call the transference matrix. Still in weaving mode, I am reminded of Schubert's marvelously evocative piano accompaniment to his song *Gretchen am Spinnrade.* In this piece the spinning wheel gathers momentum and finds a steady rhythm as Gretchen spins while singing of her unreliable lover. However, as she becomes preoccupied with painful and disturbing thoughts and feelings, her spinning slows and becomes erratic. There is a relationship, then, between the spinning and the spinner. Thus, it is not just a dogmatic use of the transference that may imprison the patient but also its neglect. Avoidance or underuse of both the transference and countertransference can be just as restrictive as their overuse since patients then miss out on what can be learned through a live experience in the room with their analyst, as well as the more intellectual learning that comes from understanding the personal resonances of an ancient story or myth.

Jung was interested more in individuation and the role of the self to promote self-experience and self-realization than he was in the social and more adaptive process of ego integration.[6] I contend that we need to raise some questions about his methods, in particular the gaps he left us with in terms of his approach to working with the transference and the countertransference.

Jung's Attitude toward Method

Reading and rereading volume 16 of the collected works, *The Psychology of the Transference*, I have been struck time and again by some of Jung's brilliant intuitions about the nature of the analytic relationship and its potential to change not only the patient but also the analyst:

> This bond is often of such intensity that we could almost speak of a "combination." When two chemical substances combine, both are altered. This is precisely what happens in the transference . . . this bond is of the greatest therapeutic importance in that it gives rise to a *mixtum compositum* of the doctor's mental health and the patient's maladjustment.[7]

Through his own experience, Jung realized the centrality of the analytic relationship and the significance of the transference as the precursor of something that is about to become conscious. However, in my view, he lacked a coherent method for working with the transference, yet it is essential if we are to treat effectively in analysis the wide variety of patients that present in private practice or hospital settings. Jung was more interested in the prospective function of symbol formation and less interested in how it worked or indeed how it develops (or fails to develop) in infancy. Nonetheless, for many of our less gifted patients and the people who have undoubtedly experienced early, traumatic parental deficits, violent families, child abuse, or chronic somatic complaints or who have a fragile or weak ego, their symbolic capacity is at best rudimentary and at worst absent (see chapter 4). Here, states of disintegration are more likely than states of unintegration. In my own practice, I have often struggled to find in myself ways of working with patients who are seriously depressed or have chronic somatic symptoms or delusional transferences. They cannot play and often cannot imagine. Transference analysis—wondering together with a patient what is happening in the moment of a session—can play a key role in helping such patients emerge from these psychic retreats.[8]

Jung was mercurial in his attitudes toward method and technique despite his interest in the self and the patient's individuality. In *Mem-*

ories, Dreams, and Reflections, he upholds an approach that tries to find what suits each patient: "Psychotherapy and analysis are as varied as are human individuals. I treat every patient as individually as possible because the solution to the problem is always an individual one . . . A solution which would be out of the question for me may be just the right one for somebody else."[9]

Later in the same passage, however, Jung moves toward the idea that method itself is antitherapeutic:

> Naturally a doctor must be familiar with so-called "methods," but he must guard against falling into any specific routine approach. In general one must guard against theoretical assumptions. Today they may be valid, tomorrow it may be the turn of other assumptions. *In my analysis, I am unsystematic very much by intention. We need a different language for every patient.*[10]

Jung's last sentence unhelpfully conflates two issues. Of course, we need a different language to acknowledge every patient's unique attributes, but throwing method and patterns of understanding to the wind is simply irresponsible. All theories change as they develop, but we still need theory to help us maintain a professional and ethical attitude. As Fordham once remarked, shunning all method is itself a method. A good many of Jung's patients came to him late in life because their lives lacked meaning. They were relatively well adapted socially and really sought an individual approach. Today, many of the patients who come to me need an analysis of their childhood to assimilate the shadow aspects of their personality. Their first aim is to feel more adapted, and they are unlikely to be open initially to the analyst's more symbolic responses.

Henderson, one of Jung's patients, recalls Jung's mercurial tendencies: "My salient memory of Jung is that he could never be put into a frame. Many people in his life tried to put him into a frame and he burst out of it, destroying the frame at the same time." I found it interesting to read about Henderson's transference to Jung during his analysis. He stated that "there was always a sense of something withheld, like a curtain drawn across a secret truth that may not be spoken aloud, something one had to find by oneself."[11]

Analysis needs some constraints that define it as a method and transcend questions about the analyst's personality.[12] While technique can seem to spoil the human aspects of analysis, I do not believe we can manage without it. We learn to use ourselves in a very particular way that includes methods of practice into which our own personality can be integrated. For our trainees, the evaluation of progress in training necessarily involves *attention* to *both competence and character.*[13]

Different Ways of Working: Keeping the Patient in Mind

Reflecting on my own clinical practice, I find that, although the transference is central to my method, I actually work differently *with* the transference with different patients. Bion said that "people exist who are so intolerant of pain or frustration [or for whom pain and frustration are intolerable] that they feel the pain but will not suffer it and so cannot be said to discover it."[14] Most of my patients feel pain. This is why they come into analysis, but for some of them, learning to suffer their pain in the presence of another is a mammoth task that sometimes lasts for many years.

In an article called "Mapping the Landscape: Levels of Transference Interpretation," British psychoanalyst Priscilla Roth has made one of the only attempts I know of to explore different ways of working *with* the transference. She contends that transference interpretations may be made at one of four different "levels":[15]

1. those that point to links between current events in the analysis and events from the patient's history (I remind you of your father)

2. those that link events in the patient's external life to the patient's internal objects (you think I am behaving like your father)

3. those that link the patient directly with the analyst (you think I am not interested in you today)

4. those that focus on interpreting an internal relationship that is being enacted in a session or series of sessions (I wonder whether my reaction is being evoked because of something you cannot yet face)

The crucial questions for me are how, why, and when do we come to choose what to take up with a patient? Roth points out that these different levels often operate simultaneously and could be interpreted in different ways. She points out that "we have to be able to allow a kind of free-floating awareness of the different levels of our experience of our patient's experience."[16] Later Roth observes that "we have to roam freely over the landscape of the patient's material."[17] She believes that the here-and-now transference relationship is the epicenter of the emotional meaning of analysis and that analysts must keep one part of their minds located at this level all of the time. I question Roth's use of the term *levels* here. The notion of levels implies, to my mind, greater or lesser depth, and in this article Roth is really comparing transference interpretations in the here and now with what we might call *reconstructive transference interpretations* that link up with patients' past experiences, the central and tense preoccupation of British psychoanalysts. As a Jungian, I prefer a multitextured approach to transference, keeping in mind as its epicenter the probability that transference projections are continually happening, each with an unconscious aim that I hope in time to comprehend. How to choose a focus may be beside the point as sometimes we are "chosen" to enact something in the transference, in the self-to-self relationship between patient and analyst. These are actions of the self rather than of the ego, or, as one of my supervisees put it recently, "listening to the stillness of the voice within, from which I could find my own direction." Sometimes an interpretation in the here and now is the place to go, and sometimes it is contraindicated. Let me give you an example:

In chapter 2 I refer to a dream of one of my supervisees' patients:

The patient is visiting a house where there is some kind of party, and someone is cooking beef burgers that are still raw in the middle. The analyst is present in the dream. Other people are given books as presents, and Bob is given a book on architecture. Bob is disappointed. The book does not reflect his interests sufficiently well. It is black and white and too rigid. He tries to change the book for something else. In another scene of the dream, Bob arrives at his analyst's house and rings the bell. The analyst does not answer immediately but comes to the door after Bob rings the bell a second time.

My initial response to this dream was that it was certainly a transference dream that brought to consciousness for both Bob and his analyst live issues about their analytic relationship. Something is cooking, but it is still raw in the middle. Maybe the analysis is still raw, or Bob is raw? The analyst seems to be too rigid (black and white about something) and was probably not hearing what Bob had been trying to convey. Obviously Bob's personal associations to his dream are crucial in trying to tease out its meaning, but at first glance it seems to suggest a need for the analyst to take up the dream in a way that is close to Roth's level 3 or 4. The dream is about Bob's unconscious feelings about his analyst at that particular moment, and an internal relationship is being *enacted* in the analysis. The analyst may well be getting it wrong and needs a wake-up call.

As a supervisor, how do I know I am right? Of course, I do not, but this was my approach with my supervisee, who seemed to find my comments helpful and with humility realized that the patient's dream indeed suggested that he was missing something—but with the promise of future engagement in the analysis about what it was. How it would be worked with was a matter for the trainee analyst and his patient, thereby raising the important question of technique.

Craftsmanship: Questions of Technique

The nuances of how analysts work *with* the transference when they believe it to be alive in the analytic relationship take us into the area of analytic skill (competence, if you like) and analysis as a craft. Sociologist and philosopher Richard Sennett talks of craftsmanship as "an enduring, basic human impulse, the desire to do a job well for its own sake."[18] He emphasizes how complicated craftsmanship can be because of the continuing conflict for the craftsperson about standards of excellence, which can be affected by peer pressure, obsession, or frustration. Sennett's ideas can easily encompass analytical psychology and psychoanalysis, as well as the ways in which analysts enhance their skills and later protect them from deterioration.[19] He contends that the craftsperson's essence is "the special human condition of being *engaged*." Analysis cannot proceed without engagement. Sennett makes a helpful distinction between what he calls "tacit knowledge" or "embedded knowledge," which is learned from good teaching and plenty of practice, and what he calls "explicit knowledge," a self-awareness about what we do and what we know, which brings with it a need to put this knowledge into words for others to ensure the transfer of knowledge.[20] The difficulty with explicit knowledge is that it is not always easy to put into words. This is something we analysts struggle with, and it is especially relevant nowadays, when what we do seems generally countercultural and needs to be clearly explained to the wider world.

Sennett uses Stradivari's workshop as an example.[21] Stradivari's approach to making violins and cellos was highly original, a factor that contributed to his difficulty in passing on his knowledge to future generations of violin makers. He could not foster in his apprentices an ability to become innovative violin makers themselves. Stradivari's house doubled as both workshop and home for his apprentices and was thus open twenty-four hours a day; his team slept under their workbenches. Because his approach was hierarchical, tasks were carefully allocated. However, Stradivari, the master, would himself add the finishing touches at every stage and was thus involved in all aspects of the production of a violin.

In the end, Stradivari's secrets died with him. His two sons could not sustain the business, which collapsed several years later. Something in Stradivari's genius was not (or could not be) communicated, and so it passed into oblivion. No one pestered Stradivari to unpack his knowledge in a way that helped his followers to find something unique of their own; the tacit could not be made explicit. How do we recover our teachers' secrets? Sennett alludes to problems of authority and community and thereby brings into focus cultural influences that can either promote or inhibit the skills involved in a craft. In an ideal world, Sennett's description of a good craftsperson surely applies to analysts: "Every good craftsman conducts a dialogue between concrete practices and thinking; this dialogue evolves into sustaining habits, and these habits establish a rhythm between problem solving and problem finding."[22]

Considerations of technique, then, owe much to our teachers and their capacity not only to teach skills but also to convey in words what they do in ways that allow us to take what is valuable in order to develop our own talents. This is not always easy, however; it thus brings into focus the role of our institutions in shaping attitudes toward technique—in this case, how to work with transference. In a chapter called "On Transference Interpretation as a Resistance to Free Association," Bollas asserts that modern psychoanalysis has lost touch with Freud's original thinking about the value of free association as a means of discovering the contents of the unconscious.[23] Bollas is often considered to echo ideas first expressed by Jung, and the theme of this chapter is no exception: "Freud is unequivocal in stating that the work of a psychoanalysis is unconscious to unconscious"— what Bollas calls the Freudian pair—which indicates an interest in the sequence of ideas even if they seem irrelevant.[24] Listening to a sequence of ideas involves waiting and casting doubt on the immediacy of some here-and-now transference interpretations.

Bollas mounts a resounding attack on the British School (Kleinians) about here-and-now transference interpretations and suggests that hearing all of the material that patients present in terms of "presumed unconscious references to the psychoanalyst" marginalizes other unconscious communications," something I, too, highlight in chapter 2.[25] This practice, he contends, produces prejudiced listening, and he even goes so far as to suggest a "paranoid listening system." Bollas prefers "now-and-then" interpretations when they come to mind, a position I agree with: "Here and now transference zealots have also denuded the transference of its variegated and diverse complexities."[26]

When it comes to an exploration of the development of technique over time, the dynamics in Bollas's own institute—the British Institute of Psychoanalysis—are particularly significant. Bollas attributes the pressure for here-and-now transference interpretations rather than now-and-then interpretations to the "view of the group." He reports that an atmosphere of group pressure among colleagues has led to the "birth, growth, and dissemination of an illusion." A persecutory atmosphere among groups of colleagues with regard to this aspect of technique evades the complexity of the analytic relationship and prevents analysts from remaining truly open and interested in their patients' communications. It "rescues the psychoanalyst from the burden of engaging in a relationship too far from consciousness."[27]

Keeping the Patient in Mind

What of my skill as a craftsperson, the way I work as an analyst, and, in particular, my own technical approach to the transference? Is it possible to be explicit about my tacit knowledge and then to find a way of communicating exactly what it is I do? To some extent this has formed a sustained thread throughout this book as it includes two detailed clinical vignettes in which I include myself as much as my patients. From my own clinical practice, it is clear to me that, for some patients, the transference is essential as a precursor of a capacity to symbolize; for others it always remains a central place of psychic experience; but for others it is to be dealt with cautiously. As Bollas remarks, "Patients create environments. Each environment is idiomatic and therefore unique. The analyst is invited to fulfill differing and changing object representations in the environment."[28]

a) Michael is the patient whom I speak about in chapter 2 and with whom I have found that working with the transference had to be approached initially with caution and great care. His dreams and my interventions have helped me to see how easily he can feel trapped or intruded upon. Moments of real contact between us, such as beginning to play together with his image of the piece of lace, are brief, and he can quickly scuttle back into his psychological cave, a lonely but private place where the viability of the self is protected. I think about the transference continually, and it helps me to locate myself in his presence, but most of my interventions at the moment focus on helping Michael understand his own relationship with his internal objects (Roth's level 2) and become more in touch with his feelings. I am aware that here-and-now transference analysis is likely to be necessary to help Michael connect with his early mental states, endure his pain, and hopefully free himself sufficiently to trust himself to make new relationships. This will take time.

b) With Sophie, the patient I discuss in chapter 3 and in whose presence I momentarily fell asleep, thereby enacting for her an experience of a neglectful and preoccupied mother, working *in* and *with* the transference is a much more fluid and natural process. She has experienced less early disturbance and damage and has a greater capacity to be trusting. Her greater capacity to bear her pain means that the analytic relationship and the transference can be a live and central place of psychic experience, meaning, and working through. We can live through events such as "the cat incident" within an atmosphere of mutual curiosity.

c) David is a patient of mine who is an extremely anxious and rather passive man and who hopes that I will provide him with all of the nourishment he needs without active involvement from him. He finds it difficult to be spontaneous and to find creative energy from the self. His dreams often offer starkly different images of women: the sexually provocative coquette, the powerful teacher, and then the musician who invites him to make music with her but on an unfamiliar instrument. These are fragments—unconnected images—often projected into me, of course, but they have not yet served as helpful links between his ego consciousness and the self. Within sessions David frequently goes what he calls AWOL (absent without leave). He disappears—shuts down—and correspondingly, I feel blank and out of touch with him. It is as if I have to find a way of encouraging David to feed psychologically, something that requires his participation. I find he needs a more challenging approach, an active interpretation of the transference as a way of breathing life into the analysis and bringing him into the room. A more passive stance from me, waiting for something in the relationship to unfold, leaves us both in what seems like a distressing half-alive state. However, the power of this dynamic has to be fully felt and absorbed into my body and psyche before I can find life and energy from within myself to offer him something. The here-and-now transference is crucial to the work.

d) Julie is a patient whom I have seen for several years on a weekly basis in the hospital out-patient psychotherapy department in which I work. She was referred after several suicide attempts, the most recent of which left her with serious damage to her body and great difficulty in walking. She is what I would call a borderline personality with a history of severe, early sexual childhood abuse. I do not work directly with the transference relationship since she is missing an internal "container" that is sufficiently robust to manage the ups and downs of her emotional experiences. She has not as yet developed a transcendent function that can distinguish fantasy from reality, inner from outer, personal from archetypal. The transference is often alive in the room; I am aware of it, and I receive it, but for the moment, my interest, my empathy, and my containing functions are more beneficial for Julie than interpreting the transference.

These brief examples illustrate something of my own method of working both *in* and *with* the transference that emerges within the analytic relationship. Sometimes here-and-now transference interpretations are crucial; at other times working with the transference on a now-and-then basis (or when it comes to mind to do so) is more appropriate. In Astor's analysis of "K" (see chapter 4), tracing the transference seemed in the end to be of no use at all.

I have pointed out that the process of individuation is facilitated by different actions of the analyst's self for different patients. I am sure that Jung would have agreed with these sentiments, but he may have been less convinced that careful attention to methods of practice, especially the subtleties of various approaches to the transference, could be valuable. This includes the complex and sometimes insidious dynamics within our analytic institutes, which can restrict our ways of working through group pressure rather than providing an institutional professional frame that allows us to develop as analysts. I believe that the acquisition of competencies involves more than a reliance on the analyst's personality alone.

Afterword

I end the book as I began in my introduction—with an Aesop fable:

> A middle-aged man courted two women, a young one and an old one. The old woman, ashamed of being seen with a man so young, plucked out a few of his black hairs every time the man came calling. The young woman, on the other hand, plucked out his grey hairs, ashamed to be seen with a man so old. In no time at all the man was bald.[1]

I hope that, on our journey to explore the concepts of transference and countertransference from a Jungian perspective, I have not succeeded in stripping these concepts bare under my magnifying glass. My hope has been to facilitate new growth and thinking and not to pull out each psychological hair until the scalp is smooth.

I believe that careful research has and will continue to help us examine our long-held theories, refine them, and consign some reluctantly to the history books. Hamilton asserts that research into analysts' descriptions of how they work with transference and countertransference affects has "moved analysis onto a more horizontal, transparent plane. Gone is the search for the mysterious, for the inner, the latent and for historical fact."[2] With reference to the mysterious, I hope she is wrong. However much contemporary research continues to encourage us to reevaluate present theory and its clinical usefulness, the search for the not-yet-known remains paramount. The knowledge we acquire from imaginative theory making in the consulting room is as important as objective data from other disciplines. We should not lose touch with this lived experience, wherein the subjective, interactive processes provide complementary, natural theory-making opportunities. We cannot separate our theory from ourselves. It evolves from unconsciousness hopefully to find a place where eventually it can be articulated. Meaning and understanding develop as we acquire the capacity to integrate knowledge that comes from outside—from our colleagues, from books, and from other disciplines—with the knowledge that wells up from within us. It is this process of finding, forming, and reforming that goes on constantly with our patients that gives meaning to our professional work and allows us to continue to assess the usefulness of our concepts and to modify them when necessary.

My approach to writing this book has been largely clinical since it is from my own practice and the diverse patients who come to see me that most of my ideas germinate and take shape. I need to get close enough to my patients to know them and yet retain sufficient distance to understand them. André Green has said that "there is no point in the analyst running like a hare if the patient moves like a tortoise. A meeting point in depth is more probable as the thread that links the two travellers also serves to keep them sufficiently apart."[3]

I am a singer, as well as an analyst. To sing, I need to be able to read the music and to learn techniques that enable me to use my voice with competence. This involves breathing properly, supporting my voice, and developing its range in both the upper and the lower registers. I also try to understand the composer's musical direction and the meaning of the poems that have been so beautifully and creatively put to music and to get the feel of how the words and the notes fit together. However, finally I have to learn to improvise and to apply my own style and emotions to my delivery. As a singer, I have good days and bad days; some songs and arias are immediately closer to my heart, whereas others take much longer to learn and integrate emotionally. Ultimately, I believe that becoming a singer is not very different from becoming an analyst.

Notes

Foreword

The quote at the beginning of the foreword is from C. G. Jung, *The Practice of Psychotherapy: Collected Works of C. G. Jung*, vol. 16, ed. Gerhard Adler (Princeton, N.J.: Princeton University Press, 1966), 72.

1. See Claire Douglas's volume in the Carolyn and Ernest Fay Series in Analytical Psychology: *The Old Woman's Daughter: Transformative Wisdom for Men and Women* (College Station: Texas A&M University Press, 2007), chapter 3, "Cherishment: A Different Way of Doing Therapy and Being in the World," 88–117.

2. Romanyshyn, *Wounded Researcher*.

Introduction

1. McNamee, ed., *North Wind and the Sun*, 91.

2. Wiener, "Transference and Countertransference," 149.

3. Jung, "General Remarks on the Therapeutic Approach to the Unconscious," 200.

4. Colman, "Interpretation and Relationship."

5. Samuels, *Jung and the Post-Jungians*, 194.

6. Wiener and Perry, "Fifty Years On," 235.

7. Eisold, "Institutional Conflicts in Jungian Analysis," 343.

8. Johnson, ed., *Final Harvest: Emily Dickinson's Poems*, 234.

9. O'Prey, ed., *Robert Graves / Selected Poems*, 89.

Chapter 1

1. Hamilton, *Analyst's Preconscious*, 2–3.

2. Wiener, "Transference and Countertransference," 151.

3. Frosh, *For and Against Psychoanalysis*, 233.

4. Forrester, *Dispatches from the Freud Wars*, 235–36.

5. Parsons, *Dove That Returns*, 67; italics in the original.

6. Samuels, *Plural Psyche*, 1.

7. Knox, *Archetype, Attachment, Analysis*, 202–03.

8. Hogenson, "Archetypes," 33.

9. Kitcher, *Freud's Dream*.

10. Stevens, *Archetype Revisited*, 349.

11. Hamilton, *Analyst's Preconscious*, 24.

12. Jung, "Tavistock Lectures," pars. 311–12.

13. Freud, "Dynamics of the Transference," 104.

14. Freud, "Remembering, Repeating, and Working Through."

15. Freud, "Analytic Therapy," 454.

16. Blum and Fonagy, "Psychoanalytic Controversies," 497–99.

17. Fordham, "Notes on the Transference," 7.

18. Astor, "Ego Development in Infancy and Childhood," 63; Mizen, "Contribution towards an Analytic Theory of Violence," 292.

19. Fordham, "Self in Jung's Works," 31–32.

20. Spence, *Freudian Metaphor*, 133.

21. Steinberg, "Evolution of Jung's Ideas," 21–39; Fordham, "Jung's Conception of Transference," 1–22. Also see Fordham, *Analyst-patient Interaction*.

22. Rowland, *Jung as a Writer*, 2.

23. Steinberg, "Evolution of Jung's Ideas on the Transference."

24. Ibid., 36.

25. Jung, introduction to *Psychology of the Transference*, para. 359.

26. Minder, "Document. Jung to Freud 1905," 69; my italics.

27. Jung, "Letters of C. G. Jung to Sabina Spielrein," 180.

28. Henderson, "C. G. Jung: A Reminiscent Picture of His Methods," 117.

29. Fordham, "Jung's Conception of Transference."

30. McGuire, ed., *Freud/Jung Letters*, 207–38.

31. Ibid., 133J.

32. Ibid., 134F.

33. Ibid., 135J.

34. Ibid., 144J.

35. Ibid., 145F.

36. Ibid., 146J.

37. Ibid., 147F.

38. Ibid., 148J.

39. Ibid., 149F.

40. Jung, *Tavistock Lectures,* para. 367–80.

41. Jung, "Theory of Psychoanalysis," para. 435; my italics.

42. Jung, "Some Crucial Points in Psychoanalysis," para. 658; my italics.

43. Jung, "On the Nature of Dreams," 281.

44. Jung, introduction to *Psychology of the Transference,* para. 362.

45. Jung, *Tavistock Lectures,* para. 368.

46. Jung, "Account of the Transference Phenomena," para. 420.

47. Ibid., para. 462.

48. Henderson, "Resolution of the Transference," quoted in Kirsch, "Transference," 188.

49. Perry, "Transference and Countertransference," 146–55; Kirsch, "Transference," 172–85.

50. Williams, "Indivisibility of the Personal and Collective Unconscious."

51. Ibid., 45.

52. Fordham, "Notes on the Transference"; "Active Imagination"; and "Technique and Countertransference." See also Fordham, Gordon, Hubback, Lambert, and Williams, eds., *Analytical Psychology.*

53. Plaut, "Transference in Analytical Psychology," 157, and "Comment: On Not Incarnating the Archetype."

54. Plaut, "Comment: On Not Incarnating the Archetype." See also Fordham, Gordon, Hubback, and Lambert, eds., *Technique in Jungian Analysis,* vol. 2, 295.

55. Davidson, "Transference as a Form of Active Imagination."

56. Cambray, "Enactments and Amplification," 283.

57. Sedgwick, *Introduction to Jungian Psychotherapy,* 63–64.

58. Jung, "Account of the Transference Phenomena."

59. Kirsch, "Transference," 183.

60. Jung, "Account of the Transference Phenomena," para. 462.

61. Freud, "Analytic Therapy."

62. Blum and Fonagy, "Psychoanalytic Controversies."

63. Freud, "Observations on Transference Love," 166.

64. Williams, "Indivisibility of the Personal and Collective Unconscious," 45.

65. Jacobs, "Countertransference Past and Present," 60.

66. Knox, "Developmental Aspects of Analytical Psychology," 57.

67. Tacey, *Jung and the New Age*, ix–x.

Chapter 2

1. Shamdasani, ed., Introduction, 6; my italics.

2. Samuels, "Transference/Countertransference," 182.

3. Sandler, Dare, Holder and Dreher, *Patient and the Analyst*, 58.

4. Samuels, "Transference/Countertransference," 182.

5. Ibid.

6. Jung, "Tavistock Lectures," pars. 318–19.

7. Wiener, "Transference and Countertransference."

8. Kaplan-Solms and Solms, *Clinical Studies in Neuro-psychoanalysis*; Davies, "Few Thoughts"; Wilkinson, "Undoing Trauma."

9. Schore, *Affect Regulation and the Origin of the Self.*

10. Schore, "Minds in the Making," 315–20.

11. Pally, *Mind-brain Relationship*, 99.

12. Beebe and Lachmann, *Infant Research and Adult Treatment.*

13. Ibid., 141.

14. Stern, Sandler, Nahum, Harrison, Lyons-Ruth, Morgan, Bruchweilerstern, and Tronick, "Non-interpretive Mechanisms in Psychoanalytic Therapy."

15. Lyons-Ruth, "Implicit Relational Knowing," 288.

16. Jung, "Transcendent Function," pars. 131–93; and "Definitions," para. 828.

17. Joseph, "Transference."

18. Klein, "Origins of Transference," 48–57.

19. Joseph, "Transference," 452.

20. Ibid., 453.

21. Blum and Fonagy, "Psychoanalytic Controversies."

22. Fonagy, "Memory and Therapeutic Action."

23. Ibid., 220.

24. Blum and Fonagy, "Psychoanalytic Controversies," 498.

25. Ibid., 498–99.

26. Peters, "Therapist's Expectations of the Transference."

27. Samuels, "Transference/Countertransference," 180–81.

28. Astor, "Is Transference the Total Situation?"

29. Kast, "Transcending the Transference"; Proner, "Working in the Transference."

30. Kast, "Transcending the Transference," 107.

31. Proner, "Working in the Transference," 96, 100–101.

32. Gordon, "Transference as Fulcrum of Analysis."

33. Blum and Fonagy, "Controversies," 506.

34. Etchegoyen, *Fundamentals of Psychoanalytic Technique,* 83.

35. Strachey, "Nature of the Therapeutic Action of Psycho-Analysis."

36. Jung, "Medicine and Psychotherapy," para. 198.

37. Jung, "Fundamental Questions of Psychotherapy," para. 239.

38. Jung, "Problems of Modern Psychotherapy," para. 163.

39. Jung, "Analytical Psychology and Education," para. 181.

40. Fordham, "On Not Knowing Beforehand."

41. Bion, *Learning from Experience,* 34.

42. Schafer, *Analytic Attitude,* 291.

43. Greenson, *Technique and Practice of Psycho-Analysis.*

44. Renik, "Ideal of the Anonymous Analyst."

45. Wiener, "Evaluating Progress in Training."

46. Caper, "Does Psychoanalysis Heal?"

47. Ibid., 345.

48. Ibid., 346.

49. Colman, "Interpretation and Relationship," 352.

50. Pally, *Mind-brain Relationship;* Beebe and Lachmann, *Infant Research and Adult Treatment.*

51. Colman, "Imagination and the Imaginary."

52. Kalsched, *Inner World of Trauma.*

53. Bion, *Learning from Experience.*

54. Strachey, "Nature of the Therapeutic Action."

55. Stevens, *Archetype Revisited,* 349.

Chapter 3

1. Warnock, *Imagination,* 195.

2. Jung, "Definitions," para. 722.

3. Plaut, "Transference in Analytical Psychology," 296.

4. Freud, "Future Prospects of Psycho-analysis," 144–45.

5. McGuire, ed., *Freud/Jung Letters,* 230; my italics.

6. Freud, "Observations on Transference Love," 164.

7. Jung, "General Aspects of Dream Psychology," para. 519.

8. Jung, "Some Crucial Points in Psychoanalysis," para. 586.

9. Winnicott, "Hate in the Countertransference"; Heimann, "On Countertransference" and "Counter-transference"; Little, "Counter-transference and the Patient's Response to It"; Kraemer, "Dangers of Unrecognized Counter-transference"; Fordham, "Counter-transference"; Strauss, "Counter-transference."

10. Jacobs, "Countertransference Past and Present," 15–16.

11. Little, *Transference Neurosis and Transference Psychosis,* 34–35.

12. Ibid., 49.

13. Heimann, "On Countertransference" and "Counter-transference."

14. Reich, "On Countertransference," 31.

15. Sharpe, "Psycho-analyst," 115.

16. Fordham, "Countertransference," 137.

17. Etchegoyen, *Fundamentals of Psychoanalytic Technique,* 269.

18. Fordham, "Counter-transference," in Fordham, *Analyst-patient Interaction,* 41.

19. Sandler, Dare, Holder, and Dreher, *Patient and the Analyst,* 84.

20. Racker, *Transference and Countertransference,* 20.

21. Lambert, *Analysis, Repair, and Individuation,* 148.

22. Grinberg, "Problems of Supervision in Psychoanalytic Education."

23. Fordham, "Counter-transference."

24. Fordham, "Countertransference," 150.

25. Samuels, "Transference/Countertransference," 184–85.

26. Jacoby, *Analytic Encounter,* 94–113.

27. Lambert, *Analysis, Repair, and Individuation.*

28. Guggenbühl-Craig, *Power in the Helping Professions;* Groesbeck, "Archetypal Image of the Wounded Healer."

29. Stein, "Power, Shamanism, and Maieutics."

30. Samuels, "Transference/Countertransference," 185.

31. Sandler, "On Communication from Patient to Analyst," 1104.

32. Spillius, "Developments in Kleinian Technique," in *Encounters with Melanie Klein,* 189.

33. Little, *Transference Neurosis,* 35.

34. Samuels, "Transference/Countertransference."

35. Gordon, 1993b, 233.

36. Ogden, *Projective Identification,* 21.

37. Chodorow, "Active Imagination."

38. Davidson, "Transference as a Form of Active Imagination," 135.

39. Schaverien, "Countertransference as Active Imagination," 414.

40. Warnock, *Imagination,* 197.

41. Britton, *Belief and Imagination,* 112.

42. Warnock, *Imagination,* 207.

43. Britton, *Belief and Imagination,* 121.

44. Schore, "Minds in the Making," 319.

45. Bollas, *Shadow of the Object,* 202–03.

46. Britton, *Belief and Imagination,* 121.

47. Jung, "Transcendent Function," para. 167.

48. Chodorow, "Active Imagination," 224.

49. Heimann, "Further Observations," 301–10.

50. Bollas, *Shadow of the Object,* 204.

51. Fonagy, *Attachment Theory and Psychoanalysis.*

52. Knox, *Archetype, Attachment, Analysis,* 143.

53. Bollas, *Shadow of the Object,* 201.

54. Humbert, *C. G. Jung,* 11.

55. Winnicott, *Playing and Reality,* 102–03.

56. Ogden, *Subjects of Analysis,* 76, 93–94.

57. Schwartz-Salant and Murray Stein, eds., *Transference/Countertransference,* 2.

58. Corbin, *Mundus Imaginalis,* 2, 4.

59. Trevor-Roper, *World through Blunted Sight,* 32–33.

60. Thomas Babington Macaulay, first Baron Macaulay, 1800–59.

61. Colman, "Imagination and the Imaginary," 22–23.

62. Jung, "Transcendent Function," para. 166.

63. Fordham, "Countertransference."

64. Sedgwick, *Introduction to Jungian Psychotherapy,* 88; my italics.

Chapter 4

1. Jung, introduction to *Psychology of the Transference,* pars. 422–23.

2. Lambert, *Analysis, Repair, and Individuation,* 154–55; Kirsch, "Transference," 197; Perry, "Transference and Countertransference," 146–47.

3. Jung, *Psychology of the Transference,* para. 425.

4. Astor, "Ego Development in Infancy and Childhood," 178.

5. Jung, *Psychology of the Transference.*

6. Kirsch, "Transference," 172.

7. Jung, *Psychology of the Transference,* para. 460.

8. Perry, "Transference and Countertransference," 153.

9. Jung, *Psychology of the Transference,* para. 476.

10. Ibid., para. 531.

11. Ibid., para. 532.

12. Ibid., para. 538.

13. Ibid.

14. Fordham, "Integration-deintegration in Infancy," 50–63.

15. Plaut, "Reflections about Not Being Able to Imagine," 113, 130; my italics.

16. Bovensiepen, "Symbolic Attitude and Reverie," 253.

17. Ibid., 243.

18. Winnicott, "Hate in the Countertransference," 33.

19. Siegel, "Developing Mind," 2.

20. Ibid., 3.

21. Ibid., 4.

22. Ibid., 5.

23. Cambray, "Emergence and the Self."

24. Ibid., 20.

25. Stern et al., "Non-interpretive Mechanisms in Psychoanalytic Therapy."

26. Solomon, *Self in Transformation,* 284.

27. Martin-Vallas, "Transferential Chimera" and "Transferential Chimera II."

28. Astor, "Fordham, Feeling, and Countertransference," 200.

29. "K," "What Works?" and "Report from Borderland."

30. "K," "What Works?" 208.

31. Ibid., 227.

Chapter 5

1. Betty Joseph, *The Analytic Encounter* (Toronto: Inner City Books, 1985).

2. Stern et al., "Non-interpretive Mechanisms in Psychoanalytic Therapy."

3. Schore, "Minds in the Making."

4. Jung, "Account of the Transference Phenomena," para. 425.

5. Bell, "Bion."

6. Cambray and Carter, "Analytic Methods Revisited," 118.

7. Jung, introduction to *Psychology of the Transference,* para. 358.

8. Steiner, *Psychic Retreats.*

9. Jung, *Memories, Dreams, and Reflections,* 153 (the page number refers to the 1995 edition).

10. Ibid.; my italics.

11. Henderson, "C. G. Jung," 115.

12. Schafer, *Analytic Attitude,* 291.

13. Wiener, "Evaluating Progress in Training."

14. Bion, *Attention and Interpretation,* 9 (the page number refers to the 1993 edition).

15. Roth, "Mapping the Landscape."

16. Ibid., 535.

17. Ibid., 542.

18. Sennett, *Craftsman,* 9.

19. Ibid., 20; my italics.

20. Ibid., 50.

21. Ibid., 74–80.

22. Ibid., 9.

23. Bollas, *Freudian Moment.*

24. Ibid., 87.

25. Ibid., 95–100.

26. Ibid., 99–100.

27. Ibid., 98–99.

28. Bollas, *Shadow of the Object,* 202–03.

Afterword

1. McNamee, ed., *North Wind and the Sun,* 51.

2. Hamilton, *Analyst's Preconscious,* 311.

3. Green, "Surface Analysis, Deep Analysis," 421.

Bibliography

Astor, James. "Ego Development in Infancy and Childhood." In
    Michael Fordham: Innovations in Analytical Psychology, ed. James Astor,
    53–71. London: Routledge, 1995.
————. "Fordham, Feeling, and Countertransference: Reflections on
    Defences of the Self." *Journal of Analytical Psychology* 52(2) (2007):
    185–207.
————. "Is Transference the Total Situation?" *Journal of Analytical Psychol-
    ogy* 46(3) (2001): 415–31.
Beebe, Beatrice, and Frank M. Lachmann. *Infant Research and Adult Treat-
    ment.* London: Analytic Press, 2002.
Bell, David. "Bion: The Phenomenologist of Loss." In *Bion Today.* New
    Library of Psychoanalysis. London: Routledge, in press.
Bion, Wilfred R. *Attention and Interpretation.* 1970. Repr., London: Karnac,
    1993.
————. *Learning from Experience.* London: Heinemann, 1962.
Blum, Harold P., and Peter Fonagy. "Psychoanalytic Controversies." *Interna-
    tional Journal of Psycho-analysis* 84(3) (2003): 497–515.
Bollas, Christopher. *The Freudian Moment.* London: Karnac, 2007.
————. *The Shadow of the Object: Psychoanalysis of the Unthought Known.*
    London: Free Association, 1987.
Bovensiepen, Gustav. "Symbolic Attitude and Reverie: Problems of Sym-
    bolization in Children and Adolescents." *Journal of Analytical Psychology*
    47(2) (2002): 241–57.
Britton, Ronald. *Belief and Imagination: Explorations in Psychoanalysis.* New
    York: Routledge, 1998.
Cambray, Joseph. "Emergence and the Self." In *Jungian Psychoanalysis,* ed.
    Murray Stein. Chicago: Open Court, forthcoming.

————. "Enactments and Amplification." *Journal of Analytical Psychology* 46(2) (2001): 275–305.

————, and Linda Carter. "Analytic Methods Revisited." Chapter 5 in *Analytical Psychology: Contemporary Perspectives in Jungian Analysis,* ed. Joseph Cambray and Linda Carter. London: Brunner-Routledge, 2004.

Caper, Robert. "Does Psychoanalysis Heal? A Contribution to the Theory of Psychoanalytic Technique." In *Controversies in Analytical Psychology,* ed. Robert Withers, 338–52. New York: Brunner-Routledge, 2003. Also in *International Journal of Psycho-analysis* 73(2) (1992): 283–93.

Chodorow, Joan. "Active Imagination." Chapter 10 in *The Handbook of Jungian Psychology,* ed. Renos K. Papadopoulos. London: Routledge, 2006.

Collins Complete Works of Oscar Wilde, 5th ed. London: HarperCollins, 2003.

Colman, Warren. "Imagination and the Imaginary." *Journal of Analytical Psychology* 51(1) (2006): 21–41.

————. "Interpretation and Relationship: Ends or Means?" In *Controversies in Analytical Psychology,* ed. Robert Withers, 352–62. New York: Brunner-Routledge, 2003.

Corbin, Henry. *Mundus Imaginalis or the Imaginary and the Imaginal,* trans. Ruth Horine. New Orleans: Spring Publications, 1972.

Davidson, Dorothy. "Transference as a Form of Active Imagination." *Journal of Analytical Psychology* 11(2) (1966): 135–47.

Davies, Miranda. "A Few Thoughts about the Mind, the Brain, and a Child with Early Deprivation." *Journal of Analytical Psychology* 47(3) (2002): 421–36.

Dickinson, Emily. *Final Harvest: Emily Dickinson's Poems,* ed. Thomas H. Johnson, 234. Boston: Little, Brown, 1961.

Eisold, Kenneth. "Institutional Conflicts in Jungian Analysis." *Journal of Analytical Psychology* 46(2) (2001): 335–55.

Etchegoyen, R. Horatio. *The Fundamentals of Psychoanalytic Technique.* London: Karnac, 1999.

Fonagy, Peter. *Attachment Theory and Psychoanalysis.* New York: Other Press, 2001.

————. "Memory and Therapeutic Action." *International Journal of Psychoanalysis* 80(2) (1999): 215–25.

Fordham, Michael. "Active Imagination—Deintegration or Disintegration?" *Journal of Analytical Psychology* 12(1) (1967): 51–67.

———. *Analyst-patient Interaction: Collected Papers on Technique,* ed. Sonu Shamdasani. London: Routledge, 1996.

———. "Counter-transference." In Fordham, *Analyst-patient Interaction,* 41–48. Also in Fordham, Gordon, Hubback, and Lambert, eds., *Technique in Jungian Analysis,* vol. 2, 240–51.

———. "Countertransference." Chapter 10 in *Explorations into the Self,* vol. 7, ed. Michael Fordham, Rosemary Gordon, Judith Hubback, and Kenneth Lambert. Library of Analytical Psychology. London: Academic Press, 1985.

———. "Identification." Chapter 2 in *Freud, Jung, Klein—the Fenceless Field: Essays on Psychoanalysis and Analytical Psychology,* ed. Roger Hobdell. New York: Routledge, 1995.

———. "Integration-deintegration in Infancy." Chapter 3 in *Explorations into the Self,* vol. 7, ed. Michael Fordham, Rosemary Gordon, Judith Hubback, and Kenneth Lambert. Library of Analytical Psychology. London: Academic Press, 1985.

———. "Jung's Conception of Transference." *Journal of Analytical Psychology* 19(1) (1974): 1–22. Also in Michael Fordham, *Analyst-patient Interaction: Collected Papers on Technique,* ed. Sonu Shamdasani, 113–37. New York: Routledge, 1996.

———. "Notes on the Transference." In Michael Fordham, *Analyst-patient Interaction: Collected Papers on Technique,* ed. Sonu Shamdasani, 12–41. London: Routledge, 1996.

———. "Notes on the Transference and Its Management in a Schizoid Child." *Journal of Child Psychotherapy* 1(1) (1963): 7–15.

———. "On Not Knowing Beforehand." *Journal of Analytical Psychology* 38(2) (1993): 127–37.

———. "The Self in Jung's Works." Chapter 1 in *Explorations into the Self,* vol. 7, ed. Michael Fordham, Rosemary Gordon, Judith Hubback, and Kenneth Lambert. Library of Analytical Psychology. London: Academic Press, 1985.

———. "Technique and Countertransference." *Journal of Analytical Psychology* 14(2) (1974): 95–119. Also in Fordham, Gordon, Hubback, Lambert, and Williams, eds., *Analytical Psychology: A Modern Science.*

———, Rosemary Gordon, Judith Hubback, and Kenneth Lambert, eds. *Technique in Jungian Analysis,* vol. 2. Library of Analytical Psychology. London: Heinemann, 1974.

————, and Mary Williams, eds. *Analytical Psychology: A Modern Science.* London: Academic Press, 1980.

Forrester, John. *Dispatches from the Freud Wars.* Cambridge, Mass.: Harvard University Press, 1997.

Freud, Sigmund "Analytic Therapy." *Standard Edition* 16. London: Hogarth, 1916.

————. "Dynamics of the Transference." *Standard Edition* 12. London: Hogarth, 1912.

————. "The Future Prospects of Psycho-analytic Therapy." *Standard Edition* 11. London: Hogarth, 1910.

————. "Observations on Transference Love." *Standard Edition* 12. London: Hogarth, 1915.

————. "Remembering, Repeating, and Working Through (Further Recommendations on the Technique of Psycho-analysis)." *Standard Edition* 12. London: Hogarth, 1914.

Frosh, Stephen. *For and against Psychoanalysis.* London: Routledge, 1997.

Gordon, Rosemary. "Projective Identification." In *Bridges: Metaphor for Psychic Processes,* 213–35. London: Karnac, 1993.

————. "Transference as Fulcrum of Analysis." In *Bridges: Metaphor for Psychic Processes,* 235–45. London: Karnac, 1993.

Green, André. "Surface Analysis, Deep Analysis (The Role of Preconscious Technique)." *International Review of Psychoanalysis* 1 (1974): 415–23.

Greenson, Ralph R. *The Technique and Practice of Psycho-analysis.* London: Hogarth, 1973.

Grinberg, Léon. "The Problems of Supervision in Psychoanalytic Education." *International Journal of Psycho-analysis* 51 (1970): 371–74.

Groesbeck, C. Jess. "The Archetypal Image of the Wounded Healer." *Journal of Analytical Psychology* 20(2) (1975): 122–46.

Guggenbühl-Craig, Adolf. *Power in the Helping Professions.* Zurich: Spring Publications, 1971.

Hamilton, Victoria. *The Analyst's Preconscious.* London: Analytic Press, 1996.

Heimann, Paula. "Counter-transference." *British Journal of Medical Psychology* 33 (1960): 9–15.

————. "Further Observations on the Analyst's Cognitive Process." Chapter 22 in *About Children and Children-no-longer: Collected Papers 1942–1980,* ed. Margret Tonnesmann. New Library of Psychoanalysis 10. New York: Routledge, 1989.

———. "On Countertransference." *International Journal of Psycho-analysis* 31(1) (1950): 81–84.

Henderson, Joseph L. "C. G. Jung: A Reminiscent Picture of His Methods." *Journal of Analytical Psychology* 20(2) (1975): 114–21.

———. "Resolution of the Transference in the Light of C. G. Jung's Psychology." In *Proceedings of the International Congress of Psychotherapy, Zurich, 1954,* ed. Medard Boss, Heinrich Karl Fierz, and Berthold Stokvis. New York: Karger, 1954.

Hogenson, George. "Archetypes: Emergence and the Psyche's Deep Structure." Chapter 2 in *Analytical Psychology: Contemporary Perspectives in Jungian Analysis,* ed. Joseph Cambray and Linda Carter. New York: Brunner-Routledge, 2004.

Humbert, Elie. *C. G. Jung: The Fundamentals of Theory and Practice.* Wilmette, Ill.: Chiron, 1989.

Jacobi, Jolande. *Complex/Archetype/Symbol in the Psychology of C. G. Jung.* New York: Bollingen Pantheon, 1959.

Jacobs, Theodore J. "Countertransference Past and Present: A Review of the Concept." In *Key Papers on Countertransference,* ed. Robert Michels, Liliane Abensour, Claudio Laks Eizirik, and Richard Rusbridger, 7–41. London: Karnac, 2002.

Jacoby, Mario. *The Analytic Encounter.* Toronto: Inner City Books, 1984.

Joseph, Betty. "Transference: The Total Situation." *International Journal of Psycho-analysis* 66(4) (1985): 447–55.

Jung, Carl Gustav. "An Account of the Transference Phenomena Based on the Illustrations to the '*Rosarium Philosophorum.*' " In *Collected Works* 16. London: Routledge and Kegan Paul, 1946.

———. "Analytical Psychology and Education." *Collected Works* 17. London: Routledge and Kegan Paul, 1926.

———. "Definitions." *Collected Works* 8. London: Routledge and Kegan Paul, 1920.

———. "Fundamental Questions of Psychotherapy." *Collected Works* 16. London: Routledge and Kegan Paul, 1951.

———. "General Aspects of Dream Psychology." *Collected Works* 8. London: Routledge and Kegan Paul, 1916.

———. "General Remarks on the Therapeutic Approach to the Unconscious." *Collected Works* 7. London: Routledge and Kegan Paul, 1917.

———. Introduction to *The Psychology of the Transference. Collected Works* 16. London: Routledge and Kegan Paul, 1946.

———. "The Letters of C. G. Jung to Sabina Spielrein." *Journal of Analytical Psychology* 46(1) (2001): 173–99.

———. "Medicine and Psychotherapy." *Collected Works* 16. London: Routledge and Kegan Paul, 1945.

———. *Memories, Dreams, and Reflections.* 1963. Repr., London: Fontana, 1995.

———. "On the Nature of Dreams." *Collected Works* 8. London: Routledge and Kegan Paul, 1945.

———. "Problems of Modern Psychotherapy." *Collected Works* 16. London: Routledge and Kegan Paul, 1929.

———. "The Psychology of the Transference." *Collected Works* 16. London: Routledge and Kegan Paul, 1946.

———. "Some Crucial Points in Psychoanalysis: A Correspondence between Dr. Jung and Dr. Löy." *Collected Works* 4. London: Routledge and Kegan Paul, 1913.

———. "The Tavistock Lectures." *Collected Works* 18, 1935. Also in *Analytical Psychology: Its Theory and Practice.* London: Routledge and Kegan Paul, 1976.

———. "The Theory of Psychoanalysis." *Collected Works* 4. London: Routledge and Kegan Paul, 1912.

———. "The Transcendent Function." *Collected Works* 8. London: Routledge and Kegan Paul, 1916.

"K." "Report from Borderland: An Addendum to 'What Works?'" *Journal of Analytical Psychology* 53(1) (2008): 19–31.

———. "What Works?" Responses to the paper by James Astor. *Journal of Analytical Psychology* 52(2) (2007): 207–33.

Kalsched, Donald. *The Inner World of Trauma: Archetypal Defenses of the Personal Spirit.* New York: Routledge, 1996.

Kaplan-Solms, Karen, and Mark Solms. *Clinical Studies in Neuro-psychoanalysis.* London: Karnac, 2000.

Kast, Verena. "Transcending the Transference." In *Controversies in*

Analytical Psychology, ed. Robert Withers, 85–95. New York: Brunner-Routledge, 2003.

Kirsch, Jean. "Transference." Chapter 7 in *Jungian Analysis,* ed. Murray Stein. Chicago: Open Court, 1995.

Kitcher, Patricia. *Freud's Dream: A Complete Interdisciplinary Science of Mind.* Cambridge, Mass.: MIT Press, 1995.

Klein, Melanie. "The Origins of Transference." In *Envy and Gratitude and Other Works, 1946–1963.* London: Hogarth, 1952.

Knox, Jean. *Archetype, Attachment, Analysis.* London: Brunner-Routledge, 2003.

———. "Developmental Aspects of Analytical Psychology: New Perspectives from Cognitive Neuroscience and Attachment Theory." Chapter 3 in *Analytical Psychology: Contemporary Perspectives in Jungian Analysis,* ed. Joseph Cambray and Linda Carter. New York: Brunner-Routledge, 2004.

Kraemer, W. P. "The Dangers of Unrecognized Counter-transference." In *Technique in Jungian Analysis,* vol. 2, ed. Michael Fordham, Rosemary Gordon, Judith Hubback, and Kenneth Lambert, 219–40. Library of Analytical Psychology. London: Heinemann, 1958.

Lambert, Kenneth. *Analysis, Repair, and Individuation.* Library of Analytical Psychology. London: Academic Press, 1981.

———, ed. *Technique in Jungian Analysis,* vol. 2, ed. Michael Fordham, Rosemary Gordon, Judith Hubback, and Kenneth Lambert. Library of Analytical Psychology. London: Heinemann, 1974. Also in Michael Fordham, *Analyst-patient Interaction: Collected Papers on Technique,* ed. Sonu Shamdasani. New York: Routledge, 1996.

Little, Margaret. "Countertransference and the Patient's Response to It." *International Journal of Psycho-analysis* 32 (1951): 320–40.

———. *Transference Neurosis and Transference Psychosis: Toward Basic Unity.* London: Free Association Books, 1986.

Lyons-Ruth, Karlen. "Implicit Relational Knowing: Its Role in Development and Psychoanalytic Treatment." *Infant Mental Health Journal* 19(3) (1998): 282–91.

Martin-Vallas, François. "The Transferential Chimera: A Clinical Approach." *Journal of Analytical Psychology* 51(5) (2006): 627–43.

———. "The Transferential Chimera II: Some Theoretical Considerations." *Journal of Analytical Psychology* 53(1) (2008): 37–61.

McGuire, William, ed. *The Freud/Jung Letters: The Correspondence between Sigmund Freud and C. G. Jung,* trans. Ralph Manheim, and R. F. C. Hull. London: Hogarth Press and Routledge and Kegan Paul, 1974.

McNamee, Gregory, ed. *The North Wind and the Sun (and Other Fables of Aesop).* Einsiedeln, Switzerland: Daimon, 2004.

Minder, Bernard. "A Document. Jung to Freud 1905: A Report on Sabina Spielrein." *Journal of Analytical Psychology* 46(1) (2001): 67–73.

Mizen, Richard. "A Contribution towards an Analytic Theory of Violence." *Journal of Analytical Psychology* 48(3) (2003): 285–307.

Ogden, Thomas H. *Projective Identification: Psychotherapeutic Technique.* New York: Jason Aronson, 1982.

———. *Subjects of Analysis.* London: Karnac, 1994.

O'Prey, Paul, ed. *Robert Graves / Selected Poems.* London: Penguin, 1986.

Pally, Regina. *The Mind-brain Relationship.* London: Karnac, 2000.

Parsons, Michael. *The Dove That Returns, the Dove That Vanishes: Paradox and Creativity in Psychoanalysis.* Philadelphia: Routledge, 2000.

Perry, Christopher. "Transference and Countertransference." In *The Cambridge Companion to Jung,* ed. Polly Young-Eisendrath and Terence Dawson, 141–64. New York: Cambridge University Press, 1997.

Peters, Roderick. "The Therapist's Expectations of the Transference." *Journal of Analytical Psychology* 36(1) (1991): 77–93.

Pinter, Harold. Program notes to *The Room* and *The Dumb Waiter,* in "Intimate Theatre: Maeterlinck to Strindberg" by James McFarlane. In *Modernism: A Guide to European Literature 1890–1930,* ed. Malcolm Bradbury and James McFarlane, 514–26. London: Penguin, 1991.

Plaut, Alfred B. "Comment: On Not Incarnating the Archetype." *Journal of Analytical Psychology* 29(1) (1970): 88–94. Also in *Technique in Jungian Analysis,* vol. 2, ed. Michael Fordham, Rosemary Gordon, Judith Hubback, and Kenneth Lambert. London: Heinemann, 1974.

———. "Reflections about Not Being Able to Imagine." *Journal of Analytical Psychology* 11(2) (1966): 113–33.

———. "The Transference in Analytical Psychology." *British Journal of Medical Psychology* 29(1) (1956): 15–20. Also in *Technique in Jungian Analysis,* vol. 2, ed. Michael Fordham, Rosemary Gordon, Judith Hubback, and Kenneth Lambert, 152–61. London: Heinemann, 1974.

Proner, Barry. "Working in the Transference." In *Controversies in Analytical Psychology,* ed. Robert Withers. New York: Brunner-Routledge, 2003.

Racker, Heinrich. *Transference and Countertransference.* London: Maresfield Library, 1968.

Reich, Annie. "On Countertransference." *International Journal of Psychoanalysis* 32(1) (1951): 25–31.

Renik, Owen. "The Ideal of the Anonymous Analyst and the Problem of Self-disclosure." *Psychoanalytic Quarterly* 64 (1995): 466–95.

Rilke, Rainer M. *Letters to a Young Poet,* ed. Joan M. Burnham. San Rafael, Calif.: Classic Wisdom New World Library, 1992.

Romanyshyn, Robert D. *The Wounded Researcher: Research with Soul in Mind.* New Orleans: Spring Journal Books, 2007.

Roth, Priscilla. "Mapping the Landscape: Levels of Transference Interpretation." *International Journal of Psychoanalysis* 82(3) (2001): 533–45.

Rowland, Susan. *Jung as a Writer.* London: Routledge, 2005.

Samuels, Andrew. *Jung and the Post-Jungians.* London: Routledge and Kegan Paul, 1985.

———. *The Plural Psyche: Personality, Morality, and the Father.* London: Routledge, 1989.

———. "Transference/Countertransference." Chapter 8 in *The Handbook of Jungian Psychology: Theory, Practice, and Applications,* ed. Renos K. Papadopoulos. New York: Routledge, 2006.

Sandler, Joseph. "On Communication from Patient to Analyst." *International Journal of Psycho-Analysis* 74(6): 1097–1109.

———, Christopher Dare, Alex Holder, and Anna Ursula Dreher. *The Patient and the Analyst: The Basis of the Psychoanalytic Process.* 1973. Repr., New York: Karnac, 2002.

Schafer, Roy. *The Analytic Attitude.* New York: Basic Books, 1983.

Schaverien, Joy. "Countertransference as Active Imagination: Imaginative Experiences of the Analyst." *Journal of Analytical Psychology* 52(4) (2007): 413–33.

Schore, Allan N. *Affect Regulation and the Origin of the Self: The Neurology of Emotional Development.* Hillsdale, N.J.: Erlbaum, 1994.

———. "Minds in the Making: Attachment, the Self-organizing Brain, and

Developmentally Oriented Psychoanalytic Psychotherapy." *British Journal of Psychotherapy* 17(3) (2001): 299–329.

Schwartz-Salant, Nathan. "On the Interactive Field as the Analytic Object." Chapter 1 in *The Interactive Field in Analysis*, ed. Murray Stein. Chiron Clinical Series, vol. 1. Wilmette, Ill.: Chiron, 1995.

Sedgwick, David. *Introduction to Jungian Psychotherapy: The Therapeutic Relationship*. New York: Brunner-Routledge, 2001.

Sennett, Richard. *The Craftsman*. London: Penguin/Allen Lane, 2008.

Shakespeare. *A Midsummer's Night's Dream*. In *The Complete Oxford Shakespeare*, ed. Stanley Wells and Gary Taylor. London: Guild, 1978.

Shamdasani, Sonu. Introduction. In Fordham, *Analyst-patient Interaction*.

Sharpe, Ella F. "The Psycho-analyst." In *Collected Papers on Psycho-analysis*, ed. Marjorie Brierley, 109–22. International Psycho-analytical Library 36. London: Hogarth, 1947. Also in *International Journal of Psycho-analysis* 28: 1–6.

Siegel, D. J. "The Developing Mind: Toward a Neurobiology of Interpersonal Experience." *Signal: Newsletter of the World Association for Mental Health* (July–December 1998): 1–11.

Solomon, Hester M. "Origins of the Ethical Attitude." *Journal of Analytical Psychology* 46(3) (2001): 443–55.

———. "The Potential for Transformation: Emergence Theory and Psychic Change." Chapter 14 in *The Self in Transformation*. London: Karnac, 2007.

Spence, Donald. *The Freudian Metaphor: Toward Paradigm Change in Psychoanalysis*. New York: Norton, 1987.

Spillius, Elizabeth Bott. *Encounters with Melanie Klein: Selected Papers of Elizabeth Spillius*. London: Routledge, 2007.

Stein, Murray. "Power, Shamanism, and Maieutics. In *Transference Countertransference*, ed. Nathan Schwartz-Salant and Murray Stein, 67–89. Wilmette, Ill.: Chiron, 1995.

Steinberg, Warren. "The Evolution of Jung's Ideas on the Transference." *Journal of Analytical Psychology* 33(1) (1988): 21–39.

Steiner, John. *Psychic Retreats: Pathological Organizations in Psychotic, Neurotic, and Borderline Patients*, ed. Elizabeth Bott Spillius. New Library of Psychoanalysis 19. London: Routledge, 1993.

Stern, Daniel N., Louis W. Sander, Jeremy P. Nahum, Alexandra M. Harrison, Karlen Lyons-Ruth, Alex C. Morgan, Nadia Bruchweilerstern, and Edward Z. Tronick. "Non-interpretive Mechanisms in Psychoanalytic Therapy: The 'Something More' than Interpretation." *International Journal of Psycho-analysis* 79(5) (1998): 903–23.

Stevens, Anthony. *Archetype Revisited: An Updated Natural History of the Self.* London: Brunner-Routledge, 2002.

Strachey, James. "The Nature of the Therapeutic Action of Psycho-analysis." *International Journal of Psycho-analysis* 50(2) (1969): 275.

Strauss, Ruth. "Counter-transference." In *Technique in Jungian Analysis,* ed. Michael Fordham, Rosemary Gordon, Judith Hubback, and Kenneth Lambert, 251–60. Library of Analytical Psychology 2. London: Heinemann, 1974. First published 1960 in the *British Journal of Medical Psychology* 33.

Tacey, David J. *Jung and the New Age.* Philadelphia: Brunner-Routledge, 2001.

Tennyson, Hallam. *Alfred Lord Tennyson: A Memoir by His Son.* London: Macmillan, 1897.

Trevor-Roper, Patrick D. *The World through Blunted Sight.* London: Penguin, 1988.

Warnock, Mary. *Imagination.* London: Faber and Faber, 1976.

Wiener, Jan. "Evaluating Progress in Training: Character or Competence?" *Journal of Analytical Psychology* 52(2) (2007): 171–85.

———. "Introduction." In *Supervising and Being Supervised: A Practice in Search of a Theory,* ed. Jan Wiener, Richard Mizen, and Jenny Duckham. New York: Palgrave Macmillan, 2003.

———. "Transference and Countertransference." In *Analytical Psychology: Contemporary Perspectives in Jungian Analysis,* ed. Joseph Cambray and Linda Carter, 149–76. New York: Brunner-Routledge, 2004.

———, and Christopher Perry. "Fifty Years On: A Training for the 21st Century, from Couple to Community." *Journal of Analytical Psychology* 51(2) (2006): 227–51.

Wilkinson, Margaret. "Undoing Trauma: Contemporary Neuroscience: A Jungian Clinical Perspective." *Journal of Analytical Psychology* 48(2) (2003): 235–55.

Williams, Mary. "The Indivisibility of the Personal and Collective Unconscious." *Journal of Analytical Psychology* 8(1) (1963): 45–51.

Winnicott, Donald W. "Hate in the Countertransference." *International Journal of Psycho-analysis* 30(1) (1949): 69–75.

———. *The Maturational Processes and the Facilitating Environment.* London: Hogarth Press and the Institute of Psycho-analysis, 1965.

———. *Playing and Reality.* New York: Routledge, 1996.

Withers, Robert, ed. *Controversies in Analytical Psychology.* New York: Brunner-Routledge, 2003.

Index

abstinence, analyst's, 46, 47

active imagination: analyst's role in, 27, 76; countertransference as, 6, 57, 75; German verbs for, 72–73; Jung's use of, 68–71, 75; and shared field in analytic relationship, 73–74; unconscious, accessing through, 71–72

affect regulation, 38–39, 97

albedo phase of *Rosarium*, 81, 90–91

alchemical imagery, 6, 25–26, 29, 37, 78–94, 105

amplification, 27, 81

analyst: archetypal role of, 23, 27; authenticity of, 47–48, 103–104; as craftsman, 112–15; identification with patient's internal objects, 61–62; imagination role, 27, 57; listening observer role, 71–72; neutrality of, 21, 46, 47, 48, 58; preconscious of, 9–10; receptiveness of, 47, 63–64, 115; subjectivity of, 22, 59, 72–73; transference role, 39, 48, 49–54; working in vs. working with transference, 44–45, 55, 115–18; working with limitations of, 99–100. *See also* countertransference; personality of analyst

analytic relationship: alchemi-cal imagery for, 78–94, 105; containing space for, 46–47, 85; as implicit interactive process, 38–40; Jung on, 45–46, 76, 92, 108; Kleinian approach, 35, 41; process vs. content of, 4–5, 31–32; shared space in, 73–74; as source for unconscious emergence, 32; symbolization in, 94–95; as trans-ference matrix, 95–100; trust in, 94–95; unconscious, importance to, 25–26, 81–94. *See also* analyst; clinical practice; patient

analytic third, 73

anonymity, analyst's, 46–47

appraisal of analyst, 72–73

archetypal experience: analyst's role in, 23, 27; and creativity of psyche, 37; Jung's focus on, 79; self as archetypal impulse, 4; self-care system, 53; transference as process of, 28, 34, 40, 78–94, 81. *See also* personal and archetypal transference

Astor, James, 43, 79, 99

attachment theory, 93

authenticity of analyst in practice, 47–48, 103–104

awareness and working with trans-ference, 73, 111, 113–14

Beebe, Beatrice, 39
Bell, David, 106–107
betrachen (awareness), 73
Bion, Wilfred R., 47, 110
Blum, Harold P., 13, 30, 41–42
Bollas, Christopher, 70, 72, 114–15
Bovensiepen, Gustav, 94–95
brain's role in transference, 69–70,
    93, 96–98
British Institute of Psychoanalysis,
    115
British School (Kleinian), 114
Britton, Ronald, 70

Cambray, Joseph, 27, 97–98
Caper, Robert, 47–48
causa efficiens, 23
causa finalis, 23
causal/reductive vs. purposive
    approaches, 23–24, 28
childhood experience: importance
    in analysis, 93, 95, 102–103, 109;
    infantile transference, 22–24,
    41–42, 43–44, 45; Jung's neglect
    of, 79, 108
classical-symbolic-synthetic
    method, 5
classical vs. developmental transfer-
    ence perspectives, 102–103
clinical practice: active imagination
    in, 76; balanced use of transfer-
    ence/countertransference in,
    106–10; case vignettes, 36–37,
    49–54, 64–68; craftsmanship
    in, 112–15; Jungian transference
    in, 26–27; limitations of Jung's
    model to, 79, 93–94, 108; session
    methods and transference, 45;
    tailoring method to patient, 47,
    103–104, 106–18; transference's
    complexity in, 55. *See also* ana-
    lytic relationship

Coleridge, Samuel Taylor, 69
collective unconscious, 13, 26, 30
Colman, Warren, 47–48, 74
complementary countertransfer-
    ence, 61
concordant countertransference, 61
coniunctio phase of *Rosarium,* 29,
    81, 85–86
containing space *(vas bene clausum)*
    for analytic relationship, 46–47, 85
content (meaning) of unconscious
    material, 4–5, 31–32, 79, 93, 102
*Controversies in Analytical Psychol-
    ogy* (Withers), 43
Corbin, Henry, 74
counter-crossing transference rela-
    tionships, 79
countertransference: alchemical
    imagery for, 78–94; amplifica-
    tion's role in, 27; author's experi-
    ence of, 51, 64–68; balanced use
    of in clinical practice, 106–10;
    complementary, 61; conceptual
    development, 57–64; concordant,
    61; creativity of, 64; definitional
    issues, 59–60, 63; embodied, 62,
    67–68; Freud on, 19, 21, 58; gen-
    erative, 72; illusory vs. syntonic,
    61–62, 64–68, 75; as implicit
    interactive process, 38–40; intro-
    duction, 1–8; Jung on, 2, 58–59,
    72–73; Jung's personal struggle
    with, 20–21; post-Jungian debate
    on, 47–49; purposive analysis
    role, 58–59, 62, 67–68; reflec-
    tive, 62, 72; syntonic vs. illusory,
    61–62, 64–68, 75. *See also* imagi-
    nation; personality of analyst
craftsmanship aspect of analyst's
    role, 112–15
creativity of psyche, 5, 15, 37, 64. *See
    also* imagination

Hogenson, George, 11
Holder, Alex, 61
Humbert, Elie, 72

idealization, 21, 26–27
illusory vs. syntonic countertrans-
     ference, 61–62, 64–68, 75
image-making activities, 26
imagination: analyst's role in, 27,
     57; concept of, 57, 105; and coun-
     tertransference, 56–57, 68–77;
     definition, 69; mental space and .
     mental function in, 69–71, 76;
     patients' differing abilities to use,
     95; unreliability of, 74. See also
     active imagination
implicit interactive process, analytic
     relationship as, 38–39
implicit relational knowing, 39, 40
implicit vs. explicit memory, 42
"In Broken Images" (Graves), 7–8
individuation: alchemy as metaphor
     for, 29, 81–94, 95; as human's
     psychological purpose, 23; Jung's
     focus on, 107; relational context
     for, 118; transference as context
     for, 98, 100
infantile transference, 22–24, 41–42,
     43–44, 45
infant-mother relationship, overem-
     phasis on, 43–44
integration, 4, 13–14, 30, 91–92, 107
interactional dialectic, 4, 38–39, 93,
     96–98. See also analytic relation-
     ship
interactive field, 73, 97–98
internal objects, 14, 41, 61–62
interpersonal relations: vs. intrapsy-
     chic approach as focus of analy-
     sis, 31–32, 79; neurological basis
     for, 93, 96–98. See also analytic
     relationship

intersubjective relationship, 43, 54,
     84
intrapsychic vs. interpersonal
     approaches, 31–32, 79

Jacobi, Jolande, 30
Jacoby, Mario, 63
Johnson, Samuel, 69
Joseph, Betty, 40–41
Journal of Analytical Psychology, 99
Jung, Carl: and active imagination,
     68–71, 75; alchemical imagery,
     78–94; ambivalence on transfer-
     ence, 2, 9, 14–21, 102; on analytic
     relationship, 45–46, 76, 92, 108;
     archetypal focus of, 79; on con-
     tagious nature of emotions, 78,
     93; on countertransference, 2,
     58–59, 72–73; criticism of reduc-
     tive method, 23–24; on empathy,
     38; estrangement from Freud,
     28; individuation focus of, 107;
     interactive model of psyche,
     97–98; letters to Freud, 16–20;
     mercurial approach to method,
     108–10; neglect of childhood
     experience, 79, 108; personality-
     of-analyst focus of, 21–22,
     45–46, 59, 79; and present vs.
     past, 23–24; and transcendent
     function, 40; on transference,
     12, 21–26, 29, 101–102; on the
     unconscious, 3, 25–26, 30–32;
     vagueness in clinical practice,
     79, 93–94, 108; vulnerability to
     transference, 2, 20–21
Jung and the New Age (Tacey), 31
Jung as a Writer (Rowland), 15

Kalsched, Donald, 53
Kast, Verena, 43–44
Kirsch, Jean, 26, 81

Kitcher, Patricia, 11
Kleinian psychoanalysis, 14, 35, 41, 103, 114
Knox, Jean, 11, 72

Lachmann, Frank M., 39
Lambert, Kenneth, 63
lapis, 81
listening observer role for analyst, 71–72
Little, Margaret, 59–60, 63
Lyons-Ruth, Karlen, 39

Macaulay, Lord, 74
"Mapping the Landscape" (Roth), 110–11
marriage quaternity, 78, 80
Martin-Vallas, François, 98–99
maternal transference, 50
matrix, transference, 95–100, 106, 107
meaning making, 38–39, 104–105
meaning (content) of unconscious material, 4–5, 31–32, 79, 93, 102
Memories, Dreams, and Reflections (Jung), 109
mental space and mental function in imagination, 69–71, 76
moments of meeting, 39, 98
multidirectional vs. unidirectional essence for transference, 34–35
mundificatio phase of *Rosarium,* 81, 89
mundus imaginalis, 74

neuroscientific basis for transference, 69–70, 93, 96–97
neurotic transference, 12–13, 61–62, 64–68, 75
neutrality, analyst's, 21, 46, 47, 48, 58
New Age movement, 31
nigredo phase of *Rosarium,* 81, 87–88

now-and-then vs. here-and-now interpretations, 111–12, 115, 116, 117

objective psyche, 4–5
Ogden, Thomas H., 68, 73
opposites: regulating tension between, 4, 76–77; union of, 81

Pally, Regina, 39
Parsons, Michael, 10
participation mystique (projective identification), 12, 29, 54, 68, 86, 98. *See also* transference
past vs. present, analytical focus on, 23–24, 34–35, 41–42, 79
patient: differing abilities to use imagination, 95; identification with internal objects of, 61–62; protection of unintegrated aspects, 13–14; tailoring method to, 47, 103–104, 106–18; valuing subjectivity of, 22. *See also* transference
pattern-making activities, 26
Perry, Christopher, 26, 87
personal and archetypal transference: and analyst's role in analytic relationship, 107; definitional issues, 12; distinguishing between, 22, 24–25; need for connection between, 31, 35–36; in *Rosarium* imagery, 90; and unidirectional vs. multidirectional transference, 34–35
personality of analyst: balancing role of, 46–49; and idealization by patient, 26–27; importance of competence and character, 110; Jung's focus on, 21–22, 45–46, 59, 79; limitations of in analysis, 94–95; and need for analyst to be analyzed, 59; and tailoring of

personality of analyst *(cont.)* approach to patient, 103; transference role of, 45–49

Peters, Roderick, 42–43

philosopher's stone, 81

Pinter, Harold, 9

Plaut, Alfred B., 27, 57, 94–95

pluralism, 10–12, 54

poetry, 7–8, 69

preconscious, analyst's, 9–10

present vs. past, analytical focus on, 23–24, 34–35, 41–42, 79

primary vs. secondary imagination, 69

process vs. outcome in transference, 29

projective counteridentification, 61

projective identification, 12, 29, 54, 68, 86, 98. *See also* transference

Proner, Barry, 43–44

psyche: creativity of, 5, 15, 37, 64; dissociation in, 30; Jung's model of, 97–98; neurological and mental aspects, 69–70, 93, 96–98; objective, 4–5; personal vs. archetypal aspects, 24; and soma, 68. *See also* self

psychoid unconscious, 68

The Psychology of the Transference (Jung), 25, 81, 92, 108

purposive analysis: vs. causal/reductive approach, 23–24, 28; countertransference role in, 58–59, 62, 67–68; transference role in, 23–24, 38, 75

Racker, Henry, 61

real vs. transference relationship, 35, 115–16

receptiveness, analyst's, 47, 63–64, 115

reconstructive vs. here-and-now interpretations, 111–12, 115, 116, 117

reductive method, 23–24, 28

reflective countertransference, 62, 72–73

regulation, affect, 38–39, 97

Reich, Annie, 60

relationship: as central to making meaning, 38–39; as developmental goal, 93; feelings vs. thoughts in, 49; intersubjective, 43, 54, 84; real vs. transference, 35, 115–16; self-to-self, 111–12; symbolization as tool of, 94–95. *See also* analytic relationship

Renik, Owen, 47

repressed unconscious, transference as expression of, 13, 30

resistance, transference as expression of, 30, 41, 58

Rilke, Rainer Maria, 101

Rosarium Philosophorum, 6, 25–26, 29, 81–94

Roth, Priscilla, 110–11

Rowland, Susan, 15

Samuels, Andrew, 4–5, 11, 35–36, 43, 62, 63

Sandler, Joseph, 34, 61, 63

SAP (Society of Analytical Psychology), 2–3, 33–34

Schafer, Roy, 47

Schaverien, Joy, 69

Schore, Allan N., 38–39, 104–105

Schwartz-Salant, Nathan, 73

Sedgwick, David, 75

self: as analyst's resource, 48–49, 72; as archetypal impulse, 4; developmental continuity of, 93; emergence of, 81–94, 95, 98, 100; and reintegration, 14

self-appraisal by analyst, 72–73
self-care system, 53
self-knowledge, importance of analyst's, 47
self-regulation, neuroscientific basis for, 97
self-to-self relationship, 111–12
Sennett, Richard, 112–14
shadow, 63, 92
Shakespeare, William, 56, 77
shared imaginative space, 73–74
Sharpe, Ella, 60
sich auseinandersetzen (appraisal/reflection), 73
Siegel, D. J., 96–97
Society of Analytical Psychology (SAP), 2–3, 33–34
Solomon, Hester M., 98
space and function in imagination, 69–71, 76
Spielrein, Sabina, 15–16, 18–19
Spillius, Elizabeth Bott, 63
splitting, 13–14, 30
Stein, Murray, 63
Steinberg, Warren, 15
Stern, Daniel N., 39, 40, 98
Stevens, Anthony, 11–12, 54
Strachey, James, 33, 54
subjectivity: analyst's, 22, 59, 72–73; as interactive process, 40; intersubjective relationship, 43, 54, 84; in theory making, 10–11; valuing patient's, 22
subpersonalities vs. repressed unconscious, 30
symbolic child, 29
symbolic friendship, 25
symbolization, 31–32, 43, 81–95, 115. *See also* archetypal experience
synthetic method, 23–24
syntonic vs. neurotic countertransference, 61–62, 64–68, 75

Tacey, David, 31
tacit/embedded vs. explicit knowledge, 113–14, 115
theoretical perspectives: attachment theory, 93; clinical practice as source for theory making, 119–20; dynamic systems theory, 98; emergence theory, 98; importance of, 109; and subjectivity, 10–11; on transference, 10–12
therapeutic alliance, 32, 35, 84
therapeutic relationship. *See* analytic relationship
thoughts vs. feelings in relationship, 49
transcendent function, 40, 76–77, 95
transference: alchemical imagery for, 78–94; analyst's role in, 39, 48, 49–54; as archetypal experience, 28, 34, 40, 78–94, 81; case vignettes, 36–37, 49–54, 64–68; conceptual evolution, 9–10; controversial areas of, 33–36; counter-crossing relationships, 79; countertransference's dependence upon, 60; definitional issues, 1, 12–14, 102; embodied, 79; erotic, 2, 15, 17; here-and-now vs. now-and-then interpretations, 111–12, 115, 116, 117; and individuation, 98, 100; infantile, 22–24, 41–42, 43–44, 45; introduction, 1–8; Jung on, 2, 9, 12, 14–26, 29, 101–102; maternal, 50; neuroscientific basis for, 69–70, 93, 96–97; neurotic, 12–13, 61–62, 64–68, 75; now-and-then vs. here-and-now interpretations, 111–12, 115, 116, 117; as pathological vs. normal, 3, 30–31, 42–43; pluralism vs. unity, 54; post-Jungian contributions, 26–28; as process vs. outcome,

transference (*cont.*)
29; in purposive analysis, 23–24, 38, 75; real vs. transference relationship, 35, 115–16; as repressed unconscious, 13, 30; as resistance, 30, 41, 58; semantic issues, 9–10; summary of themes, 101–106; unconscious as context for, 104; unidirectional vs. multidirectional, 34–35; as whole analytic relationship, 3, 26, 29, 33–34, 35, 40–45, 103. *See also* countertransference; personal and archetypal transference; theoretical perspectives; working in vs. working with transference
transference chimera, 98–99
transference matrix, 95–100, 106, 107
transference neurosis, 12–13, 61, 64–68
Trever-Roper, Patrick, 74
trust, capacity to, importance of, 94–95

unconscious: active imagination's access to, 71–72; analyst's subjectivity as path to, 59; in analytic relationship, 25–26, 32, 81–94; as central to analytical psychology, 4; classical vs. developmental approaches, 102–103; collective, 13, 26, 30; content focus, 4–5, 31–32, 79, 93, 102; as context for transference, 104; Freud vs. Jung on, 3, 30–31; Jung on, 3, 25–26, 30–32; meaning/content focus

on, 4–5, 31–32, 79, 93, 102; personal, 26; psychoid, 68; repressed, 13, 30; subjectivity of theoretical perspectives on, 10; symbolic language of, 31–32
unconscious identity, 86, 98, 99
unidirectional vs. multidirectional essence for transference, 34–35
unintegrated aspects of patient, projection of, 13–14
unintegration vs. disintegration, 108
unrepressed (collective) unconscious, 13, 26, 30

vas bene clausum (containing space) for analytic relationship, 46–47, 85
vas mirabile, 81, 85

Warnock, Mary, 57, 69, 70, 74
Wiener, Jan, 2–3
Williams, Mary, 26, 31
Winnicott, Donald W., 73, 96
Withers, Robert, 43
Wolff, Toni, 16
Wordsworth, William, 69
working in vs. working with transference: analyst's role in, 44–45, 55, 115–18; and archetypal processes, 40; in clinical practice, 37, 38, 49–54, 110–12; and craftsmanship, 112–15; distinguishing between, 104–105; implicit interactive process, 38–40; importance of both, 54–55
The World through Blunted Sight (Trevor-Roper), 74

ISBN-13: 978-1-60344-147-6
ISBN-10: 1-60344-147-6

52395